FREE Audio: For Fathers, Sons and The People Who Love Them

Discover why it's never too late to heal your relationship with your father, son, or anyone else. Learn why you can heal whatever differences you have with them even if they're no longer alive, even if they want nothing to do with you, and even if you don't know where they are. Let the healing begin...

Download or listen now at OttoCollins.com/NeverTooLate

Advance Praise for Preaching to Monkeys

"Inside this book, Otto shares many personal and heartwarming experiences that helped him know—even though it may not seem like it at times—that there is a divine order to life. Healing close relationships is one key to expanding your world view this way. This book can help you upgrade your thoughts and actions, to consciously choose gratitude, joy, love, and peace no matter what has happened in your past. And that, in turn, allows you to enjoy the greatest life you have envisioned. I highly recommend Preaching to Monkeys and applying its insights to your own life."

- Mark Pitstick, MA, DC, SoulProof.com,
www.thesoulphonefoundation.org

"[Preaching to Monkeys] definitely opened my eyes to the fact that really all we want is to know that we are loved. Things could be so much better in marriage and relationships if we made sure to convey it often instead of only in crisis. I really saw several instances that related to my life and made me think on experiences with my dad and now my sons and how to focus on things that really matter. Hopefully readers will take away that we shouldn't take for granted our relationships—family, friends or acquaintances and make an effort to show love instead of staying wrapped up in self."

- Randy Hughes

"The first chapter really resonated with me and really got my mind thinking about myself and my attitude to my kids and what my father was like. It really grabbed my attention to read more of the book. I like the honesty of your writing and am sure that many others can relate to the experiences you've mentioned. A gripping read."

- Steven Teepa

"Loved all messages of self-love and from a man's point of view! This book will help anyone get real with our feelings, man or woman. The encouragement to drop the judgment and own our accountability clearly came through. To let go of 'should haves' and 'could haves' is a big message and that we are all doing the best we can.
Great job!"

- Catharine Nimon

"You can really feel the compassion and love growing as the book moves along, as did my own understanding of how it is possible. Depending on our perception in the moment, things can constantly change. It reads very easily, and I caught myself a few times thinking of people I'd like to read it. It wasn't filled with fancy words and word-pooping (using many more words than necessary). It was so easy to digest, yet filled with juicy nuggets of wisdom in an easy compelling way."

- Veronica Bouveng

"Nothing, absolutely nothing, is more powerful than the relationship between parent and child. Give your heart, mind and soul to understanding and accepting the life-giving power of this relationship and you enter a land of profound healing. In this book, with heart riveting transparency and courage, Otto Collins places his evolving journey with his father before you. His frank, genuine and insightful recounting of his story triggers your story, forgotten places and enables you to free yourself from the unspoken bond that keeps you from your father and from loving and being loved more deeply."

- Dr. Bob Huizenga,
Author of *Save Your Marriage Forever –
the 3 EASY LOVE Laws,*
www.break-free-from-the-affair.com,
www.saveamarriageforever.com

"I think the life lessons in this book are not limited to father-son relationships, but also mother- daughter or any adult-child relationship. I think it is engaging and will be useful to fathers, sons and the people who love them."

- Joe Quinn

"I love how personal, honest, and simple [Preaching to Monkeys] is, especially with the leading questions at the end of most chapters that help the reader see their life from new perspectives and apply new things. I like how each chapter is 'bite-size', meaning that they are not too long or too short— just perfect and that you could stop reading, pick it up later and not have to re-read everything to regain context. I am glad to have read this while my father is still living, as we have grown apart ever since I left home at 18. I feel that there is a lot of misunderstanding on both sides, but there is still time to fix it!"

- Michael Carta

Otto Collins

Preaching to Monkeys

Hope, Healing and Understanding
For Fathers, Sons and the People
Who Love Them

(Also available on Kindle and Audiobook)

Copyright Notices

Otto Collins

Introduction

You're about to meet two men—a father and his son.

The father, a hardworking country preacher of modest means and deep personal, religious and spiritual convictions who struggled through life in just about every way possible and his son, a bright, passionate salesman, life coach, author, speaker and spiritual teacher who struggled mightily against turning out to be like his father, only to discover that being more like his father was actually a beautiful gift instead of something to resist and rebel against.

This book and the story that's told inside is my father's story. As the son, it's my story and I believe it's every other man's story as well.

It's about the complicated relationship between fathers and sons with real life examples of what can divide and separate us and what can heal us.

In this book, I share in explicit detail, the often painful ways I saw my father in the past and my healing and transformational breakthroughs of learning to see my dad differently.

I share how I went from having a relationship with my father filled with wanting him to be different and wanting things from him he couldn't give me to having a relationship with him of a love, peace and understanding that is rare in this world.

I also share how I shifted from seeing my father as the enemy (in my own mind of course) to being what I'll call one of my greatest teachers and role models who I totally love, respect and appreciate.

Inside, you'll read stories of love, connection, pain, misunderstanding, confusion, upset, abuse, desire, guilt, grief, heartbreak, tragedy, personal healing, transformation and so much more. You might also find some things in here that are laugh-out-loud funny.

This book is raw, powerful and deeply personal. It's the book that **had** to be written.

There will be people, especially those in my own family, who may disagree, not understand or not approve of what I've written here. They may have seen or remembered situations I've described here differently and I'm ok with that. That's their perception.

What I share in this book are my memories and my recollections only. I also share many undeniable truths about life as well as what I've learned from my journey of transformation and healing in my relationship with my father.

My intention and hope for you in reading this book is that it be an inspiration and a doorway you walk through that helps you heal as many issues, disagreements, and misunderstandings with your father or son as I did in the process of writing this book.

Blessings and love,

Otto Collins

"Perhaps the noblest private act is to open our hearts once they've closed, to open our souls once we've shied away, to soften our minds once they've been hardened by the storms of the day."

Mark Nepo

Author of *The Endless Practice* and *The Book of Awakening*

Otto Collins

Table of Contents

Otto Collins

Chapter 1
Angry Father, Angry Son

"Where did THAT come from?"

This is what I wondered a few hours after I'd had a chance to calm down from an outburst of anger that would become one of the ugliest and most embarrassing moments of my life.

I was neck deep in divorce proceedings after having left my now ex-wife a couple of months prior and a conversation didn't go so well between the two of us after one of our 8 year old son's little league baseball games.

I got so upset and angry that I threw a blue and white webbed, aluminum lawn chair in her general direction. The chair didn't come close to hitting her (or anyone else), but my getting pissed off, temporarily out of control, and throwing a chair in her direction with dozens of people watching wasn't going to win me any points for "father of the year" at the children services organization in our county.

During my whole life, I've thought of myself as a calm, gentle, loving soul who would never do anything to hurt anyone, then, I do something like this! It was so outrageous it could have upset my ex-wife to the extent of her filing a restraining order, keeping me from coming in contact with her or my son!

Fortunately for everyone involved, cooler heads prevailed and she didn't do that.

As I look back on this situation, which was nearly 20 years ago, as I write these words, I can't help but wonder:

Why was I acting like this?

And, where did I learn this way of behaving?

It's possible I learned it from my father who was a mixture of love, compassion, kindness, anger and rage. If I'd had the life he had when he was growing up, I would have felt like I had every right to be angry too.

My dad was born on March 8, 1929 and was the eighth of nine children born to Shell and Eva Collins. He grew up in a little four-room house that sat on the left fork of Little Paint Creek. It's a small unincorporated area in Johnson County in the eastern part of Kentucky on the left side of Abbott Mountain near East Point.

Not only was Johnson County less than 22,000 people but also was one of the poorest counties in America. To top it off, my father was born only six months before the Great Depression which made its mark on every town in America, as well as cities and communities around the world.

Most of the people in my father's family and those he grew up around were what we called "dirt poor." They made their living and tried to support their families the best they could by farming, doing odd jobs, manual labor or whatever they could do to survive.

To make life even tougher, my dad's father died of pneumonia when my father was only 2 years old. It left my grandmother Eva (who I only heard referred to as Evie) and her parents to raise my father and his eight brothers and sisters in that same small house.

I can't imagine what it must have been like to grow up like my father did—extremely poor, without a father, in the mountains without all the modern conveniences we have today like central heat and air, running water, an inside toilet or even a refrigerator.

Christmas was different for my dad as well. He didn't get the latest sweater, toy or electronic gadget, but instead, most years his gifts at Christmastime were nothing more than an apple or an orange and if he was lucky, a piece of candy or two.

Some people who have a difficult past let it run their entire future. They let the past dictate how they see every situation in the present moment. In my father's case, he was angry to be sure. But he wasn't raging with anger all the time like a lot of men. The trouble was you didn't know when the anger might erupt. In that respect, I can certainly see the similarities between him and me.

The only time I remember my father talking about getting violent with anyone else was when he got upset with a man he worked with on the job at the foundry. Apparently, something happened between the two of them that caused my dad to get so upset he pushed him out of an open window and onto the ground about three feet below.

At home, there were plenty of times when my father's anger got the best of him in small and not-so-small ways.

As I was growing up, my father was like god (with a little "g"), a king or perhaps more accurately, he acted like a benevolent dictator who would dole out food, drinks, clothing and shelter in exchange for obedience in his younger years and acceptance and love in his later years.

Since his interpretation of the Bible said that men were the "head of the household," my father took that to mean that it was his house, his rules and everyone who lived there needed to follow them.

In our house, my dad was the only one who was allowed to be angry.

Not my mother.

Not my sister.

And certainly not me.

When I was a small boy and did something that would bring the wrath of my father down on me, I would start crying because of what he did do to me or what I feared he would do. Almost always, in a very stern voice, my father would say to me, "Dry up that crying right now or I'll give you something to cry about!"

I also saw the "benevolent dictator" come out against my mother. Almost any time she would try to insert her thoughts or opinions into a conversation he was involved in, he would grunt out a sound of disapproval and shut her down by saying, "Can't you see I'm trying to talk here?"

Then there was the bat incident when I was 13 years old.

This happened the night we had moved into an upstairs apartment on 6th Street in our home town of Portsmouth, Ohio. We'd spent all day (and probably the week or two leading up to the move) packing and unpacking boxes, moving furniture, carrying the big refrigerator and washer and dryer up the 20 steps or so that led to our new apartment. All of us were exhausted to say the least.

About the time my father laid down in bed, the rest of us started screaming. We were totally freaked out because a bat had gotten in and was flying through the apartment.

My father, on hearing this commotion, got furious.

He got out of bed, started putting on his clothes, getting angrier by the moment and shouted, "Can't a man get a minute's rest around here?"

He grabbed the broom from the kitchen and with one strike, knocked the bat down and killed it. Then he put the broom down and went back to bed, leaving us to pick up the dead bat and somehow get rid of it.

Whether he intended it or not, the message I heard that night was loud and clear and it was the same message I'd picked up repeatedly from my dad throughout the years. It was okay for him to be angry but not the rest of us.

As the years have gone by, I've since learned that maybe I haven't always been the calm, peaceful, loving guy I thought I was. I've also realized I had this fire and anger that boiled inside me as well.

The worst part is this fire and anger would sometimes erupt at times that were completely out of balance with what might have just happened that caused me to be upset. When this would happen, people I loved and cared deeply about would stand there in shock wondering what in the world what had taken me over.

Throughout my life, in one bizarre situation after another, this anger I hated my father for expressing was occasionally coming out of me.

But why was this happening?

After all, if I hated my father so much for getting angry, why did I think expressing anger myself like this was such a good idea?

One possible explanation comes from the late, great motivational speaker Zig Ziglar, who was a huge influence on me in my 20s and 30s.

In the mid-1990s, I read a book of Zig's called *How to Raise Positive Kids in a Negative World*. In his book, Zig said something that blew me away at the time and I've never forgotten.

He said, "Your kids will do what you tell them until they are two or three years old and then they will do what you show them."

What a revelation!

Could it be possible I had watched my father's behavior all those years and somehow unconsciously become more like him than I realized?

Could it be possible I occasionally reacted from the belief that "Hey, getting angry worked for my dad so maybe getting angry will work for me as well"?

Could it be possible that the very thing I saw in my father that I hated, I adopted myself as a strategy for trying to get my way and my needs met?

Looking back, it sure looks that way.

Now, here's some good news:

Because of what I've learned over the past few years about why we humans do the things we do, I no longer get angry like I used to. I no longer allow my upsets to get bottled up inside me to the degree that they come out in hostile and larger-than-the-situation-should-call-for ways. This change in me is because of these new understandings and what Susie has helped me to see about my anger and what's underneath it.

Anger, at least at some level, comes from a thought.

If you zoom out and take a 30,000 foot view of what's going on when anger rears its ugly head, you're going to find some version of the thought:

"I'm fearful I won't get what I want in this situation."

The trouble is most people aren't in touch with their true wants, needs and desires much of the time.

Anger or any other emotion can get triggered so quickly, so easily and so forcefully within us and most of the time we don't even realize why.

I wasn't aware of what I truly wanted in the situation when I threw that chair after talking to my ex-wife at our son's baseball game.

I wasn't aware of what I wanted when I yelled at my sister-in-law while several of us were Christmas shopping one year and she was telling me how to drive.

And I wasn't aware of what was at the bottom of what I wanted when I intervened (in a not-so-gentle-way) between a father and his young son while Susie and I were vacationing several years ago on the beaches in Mexico.

What shifted my understanding of anger was when Susie and I had a conversation after reading Brene' Browne's book, *Daring Greatly*.

In the book, Brene' said, "Don't shrink. Don't puff yourself up. Stand your sacred ground."

After reading that, Susie saw my extreme anger as a way of "puffing myself up" to try to get what I wanted in whatever situation I was facing. With that new understanding, she asked me a life changing question.

She asked me, "What if there was a way that you didn't shrink to try to please others or play the 'poor me victim' and you didn't puff yourself up to get what you wanted either? Instead, what if you stood your sacred ground in the most kind, loving and solid way and ask for what you want?"

In other words, what if I didn't have to get angry anymore to get my needs met?

What if there was a better way to get what I wanted than expressing out-of-control anger? A way neither my dad nor I had been able to see. This helped me tremendously.

What also helped was learning about the "3 Principles" as described by Sydney Banks. I learned that the only thing we're ever up against in life is our own thinking. The only thing we can experience is our own thinking.

When I'm angry, at some level all that's going on is I'm having thoughts that I'm not going to get my way or my needs met in this situation. I've made up that if I don't get my way in situations where I might normally get angry, I won't be okay.

That's all.

All those times when I was full of anger, pain, and resentment at my father because of his anger, this might have been what was going on within him as well.

Maybe he didn't have any other tools in his toolbox in those moments other than to react in extreme anger, hoping to get what he wanted.

Maybe anger was what he was shown when he was young and that's what he thought was the best way to get what he wanted in certain situations.

Maybe he thought anger was the way to prove you were in charge.

Maybe he thought I was capable of more or capable of being a better version of myself than I was showing in the moment.

My father's anger could have been about many things.

What I wasn't able to see when I was younger that I can now see is that he was always doing the best he could. Even though he had moments of explosive anger, it didn't mean he didn't love me, care about me or want the best for me.

In fact, it didn't mean anything other than what I had made up that it meant.

I discovered that when I was able to start having compassion for myself, when I was able to see my own anger and where it truly came from, as well as the intensity and depth of angry thoughts I believed on a regular basis, then I was able to have some compassion for my father's anger as well.

"Your psychological suffering is simply a function of mistaking your own thought content for truth."

Dr. Dicken Bettinger
and
Natasha Swerdloff

Authors of *Coming Home: Uncovering the Foundations of Psychological Well-Being*

Chapter 2
The Dyslexic Horse

"Man Nearly Killed by Dyslexic Horse" is how the headline would have read on the internet and in small town newspapers everywhere if this situation I'm about to describe had happened today. As I think about it, the idea of a dyslexic horse is truly bizarre and the whole idea would be even more outrageous than it already is if it weren't for the fact that the man nearly killed by the horse was my father. The horse's name was Jack. He belonged to my father and as best as I could tell from what my father had told me, Jack was half-crazy, had a screw loose, or was indeed dyslexic.

The year was 1946 and my father was 17 years old. It would be another 21 years before he would learn to drive a car. In the mountains of Kentucky where he grew up, even though his only means of transportation, besides his own two feet, was riding a horse, it was also something he loved to do.

As I understand it, when an experienced rider like my father was in those days pulls back on the reigns, it's normally a cue for the horse to slow down or stop. When the rider lets go of the tension in the reigns, it's a signal for the horse to keep going; but in the case of my father's horse, Jack had it completely backwards.

One day my father was riding Jack as he normally did, which was fast, when out of nowhere a brown and white milk cow ran out in front of them. While he clearly saw the cow and would have normally known exactly what to do, he forgot. In that split second, he forgot that Jack's sense of when to speed up and when to slow down were somehow flip-flopped in his brain.

This moment was truly unfortunate because while Jack had enough speed and power to jump over the cow, he didn't have enough speed and lift to clear the fence that was solidly rooted just beyond the cow. When Jack's legs clipped the fence after jumping over the cow, they both went down—hard.

What happens next in a moment like this is up to God, the Divine, the Universe or whatever name you use to describe our Creator.

I've been behind the wheel during a couple of automobile accidents and if this situation with my dad and Jack was anything like those accidents, it looked something like this...

There is this single moment in time that seems to get stretched out into infinity while at the same time, time totally stands still—then the present moment catches up with the infinite and CRASH!

While I don't know what happened to Jack after the accident, the next thing my dad remembered was waking up in the hospital. He was surrounded by his family, praying for him and hoping he would survive. My father didn't die that day and for selfish reasons, I'm glad he didn't. If he had died, I wouldn't have been born and you wouldn't be reading these words right now.

As a result of this traumatic accident, my father ended up with a concussion, a few nasty cuts on his head, a few busted out teeth, severe bruising all over his body and a month-long hospital stay. Two of the cuts on his head were quite serious and left permanent scars that became a reminder of what happened that day every time my father looked in the mirror to shave.

When I think about this incident, I think of more than how Jack's brain was wired and that my dad could have been killed that day. Instead, I think of a deeper question I've wondered about for most of my life.

Is there really such a thing as an "accident"?

This is especially interesting to me because my sister has told me several times over the years that I was an accident— meaning that our mom and dad didn't plan to have me. I just came.

Maybe my sister thought I was an accident because there's seven years difference between us and she figured that if our parents waited that length of time to have a second child then I must have been an accident. Maybe someone else told her or maybe she just had the thought pop into her head one day I was an accident and she never thought to check out whether this was true or not.

Recently, my curiosity got the best of me so I called my mother to ask if I was planned or indeed an accident. She told me even though six and a half years had passed since my sister was born, my father decided one day that he wanted to try to have a boy. Nine months or so later, my father got his wish and I was born.

The word accident is such a loaded term in today's world. Some people who were born as a result of an unplanned pregnancy sometimes think the reason their life isn't working out the way they'd planned is because of the circumstances of their birth.

Of course there are things in your life you'd rather not have happen. Sometimes these events we call accidents are just a part of life and can happen so quickly they alter the course of your life forever.

But what if there was no such thing as an accident? Ever?

What if all the life challenges, all the people you've ever met and all the situations—both good and bad—you've had to deal with weren't accidents at all but the next step in your own growth and evolution as a person?

I've come to see in all of our lives there's perfect synchronicity. It's going on all the time and seems to be happening without our doing anything. The results are sometimes nothing short of miraculous.

What if the way your life played out was the only way it could have in order to help you become the best version of yourself you could possibly be?

What if the father you had was the exact one you were supposed to have?

What if the father you got wasn't some random act? But it was instead, a completely purposeful decision made by you or on your behalf before you were born to give you what you were going to need in order to experience the most personal and spiritual growth in this lifetime.

Having the father I got helped me by leading me every step of the way toward clarity and certainty about what I wanted in my life.

The fact that my father forced me to go to church several times a week when I was a boy—whether I wanted to or not and whether anything that happened at those churches made sense to me or not—caused me to take a look at some of life's biggest questions and seek answers in deeper, more profound and fulfilling ways (even at a very young age.).

Having the father I got also taught me about love, anger, kindness, respect and the importance of a close family, even if quite a few of those family members were a bit odd.

So are there any accidents?

I don't know for sure. But, the way I see it is, if our Creator is intelligent enough and thorough enough to give our bodies the intelligence within to heal perfectly without us needing to do anything . . .

And if the Creator is able to make the earth spin at exactly the right speed for night to turn into day every single day and at precisely the right speed so that my juice doesn't fly off the table and onto the floor every morning when I'm having my breakfast,

Then I figure the reason my father was my father couldn't have been an accident either.

When I look out at the world, there seems to be a grand plan to life that's going on all the time and it's happening without me needing to do anything except take the next step I feel guided to take at every moment of my life.

From this perspective there doesn't seem to be any such thing as an accident and there's no such thing as good, bad, right or wrong—only the thoughts we believe and continue to hang onto that makes our life experience what it is.

Just as I wasn't an accident in my family, my father's accident on his dyslexic horse may also have had some higher purpose as well.

Having the belief that there are no accidents helps me to give up the struggle and know that life is unfolding perfectly—often in truly miraculous ways—without me needing to manipulate it.

Having this understanding of life also brings me a peace that I'm okay and I'm always going to be okay even when life gets tough, I get frustrated, or when the road ahead doesn't seem clear.

"The world ain't what it seems, is it Gunny? The moment you think you got it figured, you're wrong."

Mister Rate
(advice to Bob Lee Swagger in a scene from the movie "Shooter")
[2007]

Chapter 3
When to Send Flowers

We had a party for my friend John a few months ago.

It was supposed to be John's going away party, but it certainly wasn't your typical going away party. It was much more than that.

John is one of the most brilliant men I've ever met and he has the Ph.D.'s to back it up. Even though he had those degrees, he never talked about them or the fact that he had spent his entire working life as a physicist for DuPont chemicals.

Most people spend a great deal of time wondering about normal, mundane, everyday things like "Who won last night's game?", "Where am I going to go on vacation at the end of the summer?", "How much will the price of gasoline be at the end of the week when payday rolls around?", or "How will the new hit TV show survive when the lead character leaves at the end of the season?" but not john.

While there's certainly nothing wrong with thinking about those kinds of things, my friend, John, is much more interested in spending his life taking a look at and finding answers to life's true conundrums and the deeper spiritual and metaphysical questions and truths than the average person.

John is someone I really love.

Selfishly, one reason I love him is because he and his ex-wife, Lainey, were there for me at a time when I needed it most.

Nearly 20 years ago, when I made the decision to leave my previous wife, John and Lainey invited me to live with them giving me their spare bedroom until I could get on my feet. I stayed with them for about six weeks until I gathered enough money and strength together to get my own place.

Those six weeks were a time I'll never forget—a time full of friendship, laughter, and support. It was also a time of instant manifestation on my part of everything I wanted and needed for the next part of my life.

This and the fact that we've been friends for nearly 20 years made me really happy that I got invited to John's party. John wasn't moving away to Florida, California or Arizona where so many people who've retired go to live out their days. John was really going away, as in dying of two or three kinds of cancer and the doctors had given him less than two months to live.

When our friend, Mark, heard the news that the doctors had given up and said they'd done all they could for him, Mark called John and asked if he could see him. John said because he was still able to physically move around, talk just fine, and was not in a great deal of physical pain, not only would he like to see Mark but also a few others who were special to him as well.

Fortunately, my wife, Susie, and I made the cut and we joined him and Gayle (his current partner who is really an angel in disguise), John's ex-wife, Lainey, and a few other characters who meant a lot to John for a "celebration" of his life and to have a chance to get together one final time as friends.

As strange as it sounds, between the time Mark set up the date for the party and the time we actually had the party, the doctors had done yet another procedure that added a couple more years to John's life—as if it is really possible to predict anyone's life span.

I was so glad to know that John thought as much of me as I thought of him. This party was our chance to be with John, love him, and connect with him once more, hopefully not the last time. As of this writing, John's still alive and well.

When we were at Mark's party, I was reminded of something my father used to say quite often.

He would hear of someone not doing well physically or he'd be in a reflective mood after someone he cared about died and he would say . . .

"I want my flowers while I'm living."

Flowers in this context are just another way of saying love and kindness. My dad, like our friend, John, wanted love and connection while he was living and cautioned me and every one of us to not wait until he was no longer in physical form to share it.

The idea of giving the people in your life their flowers while they're living is such a great idea, but most people hold back and don't do it. This isn't just a phenomenon that shows up in our interpersonal relationships. It shows up in how we honor everyone and everything that's important to us.

At the beginning of my relationship with Susie, because there's a 16-year age difference between the two of us, we became fearful of that age gap and what it could mean down the road. We wanted to be together for as many years as possible and we thought that since Susie was so much older, our time together would be much shorter.

Well, of course, this is irrational thinking because none of us knows how long we have on this earth anyway. The two of us learned to love and appreciate each other, as well as the people we care about, in many different ways in every moment. We've practiced giving *flowers* while the person is alive instead of waiting until it may be too late.

It can be something as simple as a phone call or text message to say, "I love you and am thinking about you." *Flowers* can also be expressing kindness and understanding when things aren't going so well or when they are. It can mean not jumping to conclusions but finding out more. What this has done for the two of us is deepen an already loving relationship and it can have the same effect in your life as well.

As you think about this idea, it raises the question:

Who do you need to give *flowers* of love and appreciation to that you haven't gotten around to giving yet?

What relationship would be enriched if you were to re-connect instead of making excuses that you're "too busy"?

There are so many ways to give *flowers* to the people in your life and we urge you to do it when the thought occurs to you—whether it's your spouse, partner, friend, relative or even a stranger standing in a line behind you at the grocery store.

My encouragement to you is to take my father's advice and give your love and appreciation while the person can enjoy it.

Your life and love will be so enriched if you do!

"Whatever shows up in your life is part of the perfection of the universal plan."

Dr. Wayne Dyer

Author of *There's a Spiritual Solution to Every Problem*

Chapter 4
Preaching To Monkeys

As I think about my father while I was growing up, I could (and did) fault him for many things but what I learned from him in a big way was how to be bold in my life.

This wasn't something I consciously learned from him and he certainly didn't make an effort to teach me how to be bold. He didn't sit me down on Saturday afternoons and give me a crash course about how important it was to be bold. He didn't put people into little boxes and label them bold or not bold.

He didn't point out how successful people are bold and unsuccessful people aren't. No, the transmission from father to son about how to be bold in a way that is in integrity with who you are was much more subtle than that.

If you were to have asked my father whether he was bold or not, I'm not sure he would have known what the word *bold* meant. In fact, as I think about one of the biggest examples of boldness in his life, I'm certain he wouldn't have thought of it as bold at all. It was something that arose naturally from his inner wisdom.

Becoming a street corner preacher was something he felt called to do, from a higher source, a calling from God, something he couldn't say "no" to.

I don't think anyone sets out in life to be a street preacher any more than a heroin addict makes being an addict a part of their life plan. It's just something that happens along the way.

When my dad's friend and fellow minister, Jim Morgan, decided to step down, my father inherited the not-so-glamorous position of being in charge of the church services we called street meetings on Market Street in Portsmouth, Ohio.

After Jim decided to stop having these meetings, my father was the one who for several years applied for and got a permit from the city to hold these gospel street meetings from 7-9 p.m. every Friday night throughout the summer months.

Market Street today is nothing more than a bunch of boarded up, vacant buildings but 45 years ago, it was a busy, bustling, and happening place.

On one side of the street, there was a Yamaha motorcycle dealership, two hardware stores, Counts Bakery, which had the best birthday cakes and sweet rolls ever made, and Hermann's Meats, a butcher shop that would put any meat department today to shame if they could take a trip back in time to see Hermann's do business.

On the other side of the street was West End Shoe Mart, Candyland, which was a novelty and candy store run by a little old woman about four and a half feet tall who always wore a white baker's hat. There were two biker dive bars with roaring motorcycles coming and going. Along with those biker bars came the occasional fights that would sometimes spill out onto the street.

In the middle of all this, facing to the east and the west were about 70 parking spaces, 35 on each side of the street. An elevated concrete pad eight inches off the ground and eight feet wide, complete with parking meters ran the entire length of the street. My dad would hold his weekly Friday night street meetings on this concrete pad in the middle of all the chaos.

Even to me as a small boy, not only was it clear they were trying to bring God to a part of town that needed it, but there was a bit of a circus atmosphere present as well.

Every week from May through September, my father would invite his church-going friends, special singers, musicians and other evangelists to hold these very loud and raucous church services. Microphones and loudspeakers were turned up to full volume as guitar players and drummers played and special singers sang.

The women who participated in the service wore beehive hairdos and long, paisley skirts that you could see a mile away and of course for men, it was dress pants, long-sleeved shirts and slicked back hair. They always gave it all they had.

And the preachers, yes there were sometimes more than one, would preach as fervently as they could until the police would roll by at 9 p.m. to enforce the curfew and make sure everything had calmed down from its earlier roar.

I asked my mother recently why it was that my father held his street meetings on that particular street and she simply said, "That's where the sinners were and your dad and the other men and women who held these church services figured if the sinners weren't going to come to church, then you'd have to take the church to them." So that's what he did.

Attendance was usually good. Some people would stand, others would sit in the 30 folding chairs my father would set up, and others would stay in their cars and roll down their windows to take it all in.

It was quite the show and as a small boy, I had a front row seat. One of my favorite memories from these street meetings was seeing one particular couple who were regulars. Just like clockwork, this man and his wife would pull into one of the parking spaces to hear the message. What stuck with me about this couple after all these years were their two pet monkeys. They were the size of seven-year-old boys and just as rambunctious.

I had no idea who these people were or why they brought their pet monkeys, but monkeys attending church services?

It's absolutely true and what's even crazier is how these monkeys acted during the services. Sometimes they'd sit quietly on their *mom and dad's* laps like children sometimes do. Other times the monkeys got excited by the music, the singing, or the fevered-pitched preaching, usually about hellfire and brimstone.

When the intensity of the service would start increasing, the monkeys would bounce around, jumping back and forth from the front seat to the back seat. The only thing missing was a rope like Tarzan might have had to swing on and their night in the car would have been complete.

As you can imagine, I was delighted by this distraction and even today, I can't think about all this with a straight face. I usually burst out laughing when I think that in addition to preaching to a couple hundred saints, sinners and anyone else who would listen, my father was in fact, literally "preaching to monkeys."

But to my father, these services on Market Street weren't a circus or a sideshow. They were something he was serious about. It was a sacred act. In his mind, he was doing what he could to bring lost souls to God.

Personally, I was both embarrassed and intrigued by the fact that my father was out on the streets preaching the gospel.

I was embarrassed and could only imagine what all these people who came to Market Street during these services were thinking. Some of them would circle the block dozens of times looking from a distance at the sideshow that was going on.

But I was also intrigued because of the music, the bands, the singers, the excitement and the passion that was on display Friday night after Friday night throughout the entire summer.

This, dear reader, as I look back on it now, was my father being bold and ballsy.

In order to organize these church services and preach in this manner, my father had to not care what his co-workers or foreman might say to him on Monday morning at the foundry. He had to not care what people might think if he ran into them at the grocery store. He had to ignore what might be said to his family about his unusual calling as a street corner preacher.

I've often wondered about my father's preaching on the streets and whether he was ever fearful or filled with anxiety. This is a question I'll never know the answer to and over the years I've certainly thought about it and here's why:

In about any published survey, fear of public speaking usually comes in second as the biggest fear most people have, right below the fear of dying.

Several times a week when I was growing up, I would see my father preaching from a pulpit, not only on the street corners but in various churches as well. He would speak confidently and express his thoughts, ideas, and beliefs and share what he was passionate about in front of tens or hundreds of people. This happened so often that I came to see speaking in public as something that's normal.

It's also one of the reasons I've never thought speaking was something to be fearful about. I saw it as something just as normal and natural as the sun coming up and setting again each day.

Because of my father's example, I've done a lot of things that many people might consider to be bold and ballsy in my life as well.

I got my first job selling radio advertising when I was 18. I started my own advertising agency when I was 24. Along with my wife, Susie, we started our relationship and life coaching practice, simply sharing from our hearts what was working for us in our relationship when I was 37 with no psychology degree.

I've been willing to let go of many things that changed the course of my life and I've been willing to say "yes" to many more that have helped me to create the life I have today.

And best of all, I'm not done yet which brings me to an interesting point about boldness that so many people wonder about:

What does boldness look like?

What does it take to be bold?

And where in your life do you want to be a little bit or a lot bolder?

To me, boldness doesn't look like anything you ordinarily might think it does. It's usually much more subtle like how my father passed down the trait of boldness just by me observing his life.

Being bold isn't usually something that's intentional. You don't get up in the morning and start chanting in the mirror when you're shaving about all the ways you're going to be bold today. It's not puffing yourself up to be someone you're not.

No, being bold is just saying "yes" to the life you want. Being bold is a million little decisions that add up to a life well-lived as you look in the rear-view mirror of years gone by.

When I was younger, I would never have thought of my father as bold. Now, as I look back on his life, I can plainly see that he was.

As I write this, I am thinking about all the times I didn't see my father's boldness, but instead focused on the hurt, embarrassment, and all the ways I wanted him to be different.

Now, I'm starting to see through new eyes and I'm seeing him in new ways. I'm appreciating all the gifts he gave to me that I never saw in my earlier years.

Boldness is just one of them.

"We honor our parents by carrying their best forward and laying the rest down. By fighting and taming the demons that laid them low and now reside in us. It's all we can do if we're lucky."

Bruce Springsteen

Author of *Born to Run*

Chapter 5
The Rebellion Begins

As far back as I can remember, curiosity has always been one of my constant companions and my mother says I couldn't have been more than three years old when my curious streak really started to reveal itself in earnest.

My mother, father, sister and I lived in a small rented house at 816 Court Street on the south end of the small town of Portsmouth, Ohio where I grew up. We lived exactly one half block from the palatial, granite, Scioto County Courthouse and a half block north of Scudder Elementary School where I attended until the 3rd grade.

As an adult, with the exceptions of a few speeding tickets I've been gifted with by various state highway patrol officers who thought I was going a little faster than the speed limit— and a party I had one weekend when I was eighteen that got a little too loud and a little too out-of-control for our neighbor's taste when my parents were out of town visiting my aunt and uncle in Toledo one hot August weekend, I've never had any run-ins with the law at all.

But as a three-year-old boy, the police regularly came calling to pay me a visit, all because of my passion, desire and innate curiosity.

I've always loved to drive a car and it's a very short list of things I enjoy doing more than getting behind the steering wheel of a car, pushing the accelerator down with my right foot and taking off.

Two houses south of where we lived was a dirt and gravel parking lot where the teachers and administrators of the elementary school a half a block away parked their cars. Day after day, week after week, when I woke from my afternoon nap, I would somehow manage to sneak away from my mother and worm my way unseen down to the school parking lot where all these amazing cars were parked. I'd love to be able to go back in time to see how I actually did it, but what happened next was always thrilling for a small boy like me to say the least.

This was long before power door locks and remote control key fobs that keep our cars of today more secure. I would find a car or truck that wasn't locked, climb up in it, lock the doors behind me, stand up on the driver's seat, grab hold of the steering wheel and start pretending to drive. I'd do this all afternoon until I was caught, either by my mother, the neighbors, or finally the owners of the vehicle I had just taken over.

Most of the time, my father was at work in the blistering heat of the foundry and missed most of these adventures.

Nobody could get me out of the cars or trucks I'd taken over, because once I realized the owners of the vehicles were trying to unlock the doors to get me out, I'd stop them. As they tried to unlock the door with the keys to the vehicle, I'd push down on the locks and relock the door really quickly over and over. Quite often, I'd keep my little "driving party" going long enough that the city police had to be called and play the authority trump card to help get me out of the car.

This was just one of many ways my curiosity would lead me on some grand adventure and with my curious streak well under way, my rebellious phase would only be a few short years ahead.

Curiosity can cause you to think, to wonder, to doubt, to explore, to dig deep, and to look at things in new ways.

Curiosity can lead to new excitement and a passion-filled life and sometimes curiosity can lead you to discover things you'd rather not have found out.

Curiosity can also lead to rebellion and one of the things I've found to be true about life is that almost everyone rebels against something. The trouble is that most of us go through our lives not knowing what that something truly is and how it affects us—sometimes until it's too late.

An example of this is how common it is for kids to rebel against their parents, teachers, or anyone they perceive to be an authority figure.

It happens all the time and I was no different.

We all always do whatever makes sense to us in the moment given our current level of thinking.

So often young people reach a point in their lives where they think the answers to all the problems they've dreamed up would somehow be magically solved if their parents, caregivers or other authority figures were or weren't a certain way.

As a result of this faulty thinking, they get this fervent desire to break away from mom, dad, the family, or the system and what they think about what's expected of them. They find some way to rebel and start to individuate through whatever means necessary to become their own person.

This rebellion can be big or small and can take all kinds of forms in a person's life.

Drugs, sex, rock n' roll, moving far away, fighting, going to a different university than your parents would like you to, dropping out of school completely, or becoming a vegetarian or a meat-eater when your family culture is different. It might mean becoming a fireman when the family business is something else or not attending family holidays just because it's expected, and on and on.

To be sure, I've had my share of disagreements and differences with my mother throughout my life but my rebellion took another turn.

First as a small boy and later as a young man, even though I wasn't fully aware of what I was doing at the time, I decided I would choose to spend my time, energy and thoughts rebelling against my father, the church, and last but not least, GOD.

The reasons I chose these three targets to rebel against will become clear in a moment but it's safe to say that I've always been someone who's had a strong will and his own unique way of looking at life.

Starting at the time of my birth and up until my final rebellion, I was forced by my father to attend church services three to seven days a week. Going to church was by far the most important thing in my father's life.

It was Work. Eat. Go to church. Sleep.

Day in, day out. Week in, week out. Go to church—that's what we'd do in our family. Not only was this expected of everyone, but it was mandatory.

Our churches were small in comparison to most churches you see in small towns and in more rural areas of today. The attendance was small. 20 to 50 people would be a normal crowd. At a revival or all-day meeting with dinner-on-the-grounds, you'd see 75 to 100 or more attend those special services. Except for Sunday school, most services would begin at 7:30 in the evening. This gave the members of the church or the flock, the singers, deacons, and the designated man who was bringing the message that evening time to get a bath, put on their best clothes, get a bite to eat, and still get to the service on time after a long, hard day at work.

The men giving the message weren't called ministers. They were called preachers and that's what they would do at the end of every church service—preach.

My dad was one of them. Even though he was ordained as a minister at the People's Tabernacle Church one Saturday night along with a few other men, if asked, he wouldn't have said he was a minister.

He would have stood tall and confidently told you he was "called" to preach and ordained by God to do His work.

And what subject would these preachers like my dad preach about most nights?

Hellfire and Brimstone!

The preacher for the night would get on a stage, known as a pulpit, and essentially spend the next half hour trying his best to scare the shit out of you by talking about all the bad stuff that was going to happen to you that included hellfire and brimstone, if you didn't turn your life over to Jesus Christ and accept him as your personal Savior right now.

The way I understood how this hellfire and brimstone thing worked was if you died or Jesus came back to earth before you accepted him as your Lord and Savior, it would essentially mean, game of life over. Thanks for playing. You would not pass go, you would not collect $200 like in the game of Monopoly, but you would go straight to Hell and you'd burn in a lake of fire forever—all because you didn't accept Jesus as your Lord and Savior.

This was serious stuff and even though it's been about 50 years ago, I remember like it was yesterday and here's the problem:

Throughout my life, this just hasn't made any sense to me.

I mean, my bullshit meter was getting pegged all the way to the right every time I would hear these hellfire and brimstone messages.

I couldn't stomach the idea of believing that if there is such a thing as a God—which I believe there is—that God would damn one of his children to burn in a lake of fire forever regardless of what a person believed or what they did wrong in life.

I just couldn't fathom it.

I still can't.

Even as a small boy, I had a *knowing* there indeed was such a thing as a powerful, all-knowing God, but there was no way he, she or it was this angry, evil, pissed off being that was so domineering and egotistical that he just wanted to make his children's lives miserable after they left this earthly plane.

It would be like a man who was upset because his child had some sort of memory loss and couldn't remember who he was. He wouldn't want to kill his child or torture him forever just because he couldn't see the truth that there was a Creator.

Even as a small child, the God I knew was a kind, loving God who wanted the best for his children.

He wasn't angry, evil or vindictive.

Those are the kinds of things I imagine Satan would be like if there really was such a thing.

And that's why I rebelled against religion, God, going to church, my father, and anything and anyone who wanted me to believe in something that didn't feel right and true.

In his later years, even though he had mellowed a great deal, my father's greatest wish, more than anything else I believe, was for me to go to church with him.

We would have many meaningful conversations over the years about important things, but I don't think he ever completely understood how deep our differences were about this issue.

Even though it was perhaps my father's greatest desire, other than attending a wedding or a funeral, I never once attended a church service with my father after I was 17 years old. I couldn't do it—not even once.

Common Ground

I couldn't see it at the time because we always see things we need to see in our own time (maybe it's more like God's time) but as I look back on it, there was a big shift, a softening, an acceptance, a deeper feeling of love that happened between my father, my mother and me when I was 35.

It was when my first marriage of 15 years was ending and boy, did it end badly.

There aren't many things about my life I regret but two of them are biggies.

One is the way my first marriage ended and the fact that I didn't have the skills at the time to navigate through the treacherous and uncharted waters of ending a relationship with someone I loved in a kind, honoring and respectful way.

The second that's equally as big is that because I was the one who left the marriage, I missed a lot of experiences with our son since he was eight years old when I left.

You can never go back in life, you can never know what the future has in store for you, and you can also never know what the BIG GUY (AKA God or The Great Spirit) has planned for you and this period of my life was showing me that in living color.

Not only was I in the middle of a separation and divorce, but it was also the beginning of a time of great learning, expanding, and growing personally and spiritually.

Ever since I was a small child, I've spent more time than I can recall wondering about three of life's biggest questions:

Who am I?

Why am I here?

What's this all about?

As the years go by, the answers to these questions continue to drive me, humble me, and open me to life and to love in ways I could never have imagined in my early years. More and more I'm interested in living from the place inside me that's inside all of us—the divine—the beautiful—the sacred.

When I think about these questions, I'm reminded of one of my favorite quotes from the late business philosopher, Jim Rohn, who was a big influence on me when I first started my personal growth and spiritual development journey. While I don't agree with the bulk of Jim's philosophy today, I'll bet I heard one particular recording a hundred times of a talk he gave.

In the talk Jim said, "The Bible gives us a list of human stories on both sides of the ledger. On the list of human stories that were used were examples—Do what these people did. Another list of human stories used in the Bible was warnings—Don't do what these people did. So if your story ever gets in one of these books, make sure they use it as an example, not a warning."

When I was young, I thought I had all the answers to life. Back then, I thought of my father, his life and the decisions he made as a warning to me and to others.

In those days, when I looked at my father's life and saw how he lived and what was important to him, it was like big flashing red lights in my head shouting. . .

"Don't live like this. Don't be like this and don't think like this. You'll be miserable, broke and unfulfilled if you do."

I remember going to a psychologist a few weeks after I left my first marriage to get some help making sense of all the changes that were going on in my life at that time. After we'd been talking about Dad in one of the earlier sessions, the counselor looked at me, smiled, and then winked at me playfully and said, "You'd better be careful or you'll end up like your father."

Now that my dad's gone, I can see what that counselor meant.

As I am now able to look back at my dad through fresh eyes, I can see him and his life as an example and not a warning, because I'm open to seeing it that way.

I've come to realize that like anything in life, you can always find what you go looking for.

So many people spend their whole lives rebelling, pushing against, and fighting the very things they want most in life. They rebel against their lover when they want love. They rebel against freedom when they want freedom. They rebel against health when they want health. They rebel against money when they want money. It doesn't make any sense, but that's what we as humans do. We rebel and think it will get us what we want.

Lovers love, fighters fight, and rebels rebel.

I rebelled because I thought MY WAY was the way and my father's way wasn't.

I rebelled because I thought there was only one right and one wrong way to live, to be and to see things. I thought I was right and my father was wrong. I thought I had to rebel to be my own person, to feel important and to be a man, even before I was ready. I rebelled because, like anybody who does what they do, I thought it was the best way to feel important, special and to get my needs met.

As the years passed, I've learned some very important life lessons. Because of what I've learned, I've softened and in his later years so did my father.

As I said in the beginning of this chapter, we ALL rebel against something.

The question is what?

And why?

Lately, I've learned I don't have to be a rebel or push or rail against what I don't want—to get what I *do* want in life.

I wish I'd seen this earlier. If I had, I might have been able to avoid some of the bumps, bruises, headaches and heartaches I've experienced as I've traveled along life's highway.

"Forgiveness doesn't come
with a debt."

Mary Chapin Carpenter

Singer-Songwriter

Chapter 6
The Last Punishment

Today, my father would probably have been put in jail many times for what he did to my sister and me as a way of disciplining us for what we had done *wrong* as kids.

But times have changed since then and the rules for parenting, child-raising, and what is acceptable and what isn't were far different when I was a child than they are now. I was beaten with a belt or his hand far too many times to remember.

I loved my father, but as a small child, I always felt that I'd never done anything that would warrant the kind of punishment he sometimes gave me.

No one does.

I don't remember all of my childhood. But one thing that stands out is the last beating I got from my dad with his belt.

It was the summer after I had finished the eighth grade, which would mean I was 13 years old, soon to be 14. We had just moved to a new house (again) a few months before and I hated it.

I hated that we had just moved from the neighborhood where we had lived the longest which was about four and a half years. But what I really hated was why we moved.

Please understand this is only my perspective, but as I saw it, there was only one reason why we moved from the nicest house we'd ever lived in, the neighborhood I loved and the place where all my friends were.

It was because of Mrs. Daubbs.

Mrs. Daubbs lived next door to us with her husband, John, and seemed to me to be as mean as a snake and I thought she needed to be treated as such.

I tried to do my part to treat her the way I thought she should be treated. I'd throw rocks at her dogs and bust glass bottles on her front porch as I walked by on a summer day. The only thing that happened as a result of what I did was me getting to blow off a little steam.

Often, as my father was walking from his car to the house after a long day of work at 11 p.m., Mrs. Daubbs would cuss at him for no reason and spray him with water from her garden hose while watering her seven foot hedges. Eventually, my father let her antics drive us from our home and out of the neighborhood.

Even though the neighborhood where we moved was only five miles away from where we lived before, it felt like 5,000 miles because the friends I played with every day were gone.

Well, they weren't gone. They were where they'd always been but I wasn't there with them anymore and it hurt me to the bone. I didn't know how to deal with the fact that my best friends and all the people I spent time with were gone.

I tried to make new friends, but the combination of changing schools in the middle of the year, riding a school bus for the first time, and being in a new neighborhood where the other kids, especially boys, didn't want much to do with me made me miserable to say the least.

This is when I started drinking alcohol as a 13-year-old eighth grader because three of the boys in the neighborhood who finally did seem to like me all drank.

After school, my new friends, Steve, John and Paul and I would play baseball in the field below our house near the creek. We'd play until we either lost the ball in the weeds or the creek, it got too dark to see, or one of us would get called home. At our young ages, none of us had much money and we were all underage, so, we had to enlist the help of a willing accomplice to buy our booze for us.

Luckily, or perhaps not so luckily depending on how you look at it, we had a guy in his early 20s who rode a motorcycle move into a house a few doors away and he'd run to the carry-out and buy us whatever we wanted.

All we had to do was ask and he'd hop on his Yamaha motorcycle and be back in a flash. Boones Farm wines along with Schlitz and Miller beers were our drinks of choice on those nights when we'd all sneak out of our houses, meet up at our booze-buying friend's house or down the road in the woods and drink what we had.

Because I was often bored and usually looking for things to do when I wasn't with my new friends, I would sometimes go to the foundry where my father worked in the early evening and stay with him until he got off work at 11 p.m. While I was there, I would spend my time going back and forth between watching him work and getting into things I shouldn't and then I'd ride home with him.

I did this many times but on one particular day, my mother was in the hospital having a medical procedure done and I was spending my day with some other friends. They were actually family because those boys were the brothers of my sister's husband.

My agreement with my father was that I was supposed to be at his work when he took his dinner break at 9:00 p.m. Because it was summer and it didn't get dark until much later than normal at that time of year, I lost all track of time as boys sometimes do.

I instantly knew I was in deep trouble when I looked at a clock and realized I was already late. My father's dinner break would soon be over and I wasn't there.

Not knowing what to do, I took off running as fast as I could toward the Portsmouth Casting Company where my father worked and prepared for what I knew was coming—to get the shit beaten out of me.

I wasn't wrong.

When I arrived at the big open door of the foundry, I was hit by the heat of the iron castings as it was being escorted out of the building by giant fans. As I weaved my way through department after department of the foundry to get to where my dad was, I felt like I was marching into my own death.

Maybe he was just scared that I was hurt. Maybe he was angry. Maybe he wanted to teach me a lesson. Maybe his thoughts got away from him and he didn't know how to deal with his rebellious son in the moment.

Whatever his reason, it doesn't really matter now.

When I got to where my father was, he took off his belt and whipped me with it five or six times. I don't remember exactly how many times, but what I do remember is how badly it hurt and how much I hated him for doing that to me for just forgetting about the time.

As a result of him beating me like that, I made a decision. I swore that would be the last time he ever beat me and if I ever had children, I'd NEVER do anything like that to them.

I didn't deserve a beating like that and neither does anyone else.

The only time I ever raised my hand to my son was one Saturday afternoon when he was five years old and we were shopping. My son's mother had stayed home that day and it was just the two of us boys. As we were leaving one of our favorite stores, I asked him on the way out if he had to pee and he said no.

Two minutes later, he peed right in his pants. We were almost to our car and I lost it. I don't know what happened in that moment, but when I saw him peeing right after I had just asked him if he had to go, for some reason I just snapped. Before I knew what I was doing, I swatted him two or three times on his behind with my bare hand.

Hard.

Just like what my dad had done to me, I punished my son in a manner he didn't deserve. As the saying goes, it hurt me way more than it hurt him and that was pretty bad.

I don't know if my son remembers this and if he does, I sometimes wonder, does it still hurt?

Over the years, I've wondered if he is holding onto any leftover resentment from that traumatic day.

Whether he remembers anything from that day or not, something important happened to me as a result of that moment.

I made a promise to myself that I'd never mistreat or physically hurt my son in any way ever again and except for the time I unintentionally hit him in the head with a baseball when we were playing catch in the too-dark-to-be-playing-ball evening, I've kept that promise.

For a while, I didn't know if I could forgive myself for what I had done to my son on that boys' day out but 20 years later, I eventually did.

I think I forgave my father on that day too.

Forgiveness is such a funny thing.

You can go through your whole life and not realize you haven't forgiven others, or more importantly, you haven't forgiven yourself for something. The crazy thing is that most of the time you're the only one stuck in the tar and the only one suffering from the pain of unresolved hurt.

Sometimes, the other person who you've been upset with, angry at, or unwilling to make amends with is completely unaware of how much you're still holding onto something that's causing you and that other person to feel distant, separated and disconnected.

I remember a time a few years ago when a very well-known colleague of mine wanted Susie and me to be partners on a project of his. After the whole thing fell apart, I was so emotionally invested in it that I burned inside with anger and held onto that anger for all these years. The way the whole thing ended still burns inside me.

If I'm truthful about it, the reason I've held onto the pain of that situation so long is because I haven't forgiven myself for not seeing it more clearly, not understanding what our colleague really wanted from us, and the thought that I should have known better. I felt like I shouldn't have taken the whole thing so personally, but I did.

Forgiveness—or the feeling you need to forgive someone or there's something that needs to be forgiven—is all just thought. You can get stuck in a loop of thinking that can make you miserable, especially the thought that something or someone did you wrong, they need to acknowledge they did wrong, and let you know how sorry they are.

It's made me miserable for far too long about a situation that the other person has probably long forgotten.

Maybe it's time to forgive him, or better yet, let those thoughts that I need to forgive him come and go when they come up within me.

Maybe these thoughts are just thoughts and I don't need to forgive at all.

Maybe I need to live more in the present moment.

Maybe I need to love myself more and see that I, along with everyone else, am always just doing the best I know how to do in every moment.

Let's fast-forward a few months in time, after I wrote the first part of this chapter to a conversation I had with my mother about my father, Mrs. Daubbs, and why we moved from that house and neighborhood I loved so much.

My mother lives in Portsmouth, Ohio which is the same small town I grew up in and it's about a two hour drive from where I live now. I try to see her about once a month, but sometimes life gets in the way and I don't make it so a phone call or two has to do.

One particular Sunday, I had driven the two hours to see her and I don't know why but at one point when there was a lull in the conversation, I asked her if she remembered why we moved from that small five-room house on Bertha Avenue next to Mrs. Daubbs.

To say that her answer to my question totally rocked my world would be an understatement.

She told me the reason my father decided we should move from that neighborhood that I loved so much was to protect me.

That's right. We moved to protect ME from Mrs. Daubbs.

You see, I didn't find out the truth until that Sunday 38 years later when I asked my mother about all this. She told me that Mrs. Daubbs accused me of trying to kill her dogs and poison her hedges. Because of this, Mrs. Daubbs, in return, did the kinds of things I described earlier to retaliate for what she believed I did.

I didn't do what she accused me of doing but on this Sunday afternoon talking with my mother, a still deeper level of forgiveness washed over me towards my father about all this.

Isn't this the way it works so often in life?

We think about something a certain way, sometimes for years or maybe our whole life, and then we have an insight that it wasn't really the way we thought it was at all. It was totally different; we just didn't or couldn't see it at the time.

For nearly 40 years, I thought the reason we moved was because my father was being a victim, a wimp, or pushover and he let that woman get the best of him.

When I think about all this now, I sometimes wish my father was still here so I could say I'm sorry for all the years I thought badly about him for what he did. I'd also want to tell him how much I appreciate him for taking up for me and for wanting to protect me.

As I close out this chapter, here are a few questions to consider spending some time with the next time you have a quiet moment alone:

When have you thought about something and thought it was one way only to find out later that it was another?

Have you ever found that how you thought about a certain situation wasn't the way it really was at all?

Have you ever had a situation in your life that you wished you could go back in time and change but because of circumstances, it's not possible?

What do your answers about these questions mean for you in your life?

While I can't go back and thank my father, I can make sure I don't make the same mistake in the future, allowing myself to jump to conclusions about a situation until I have the facts and focusing on thoughts that create separation from those I love.

"It's the parents in our head
that are the problem."

Annie Lalla

Cartographer of Love

Chapter 7
Learning to Love Junior

There were nine kids, six girls and three boys, in my father's family when he was growing up.

Every one of my dad's brothers and sisters except one had really weird "O" names. On the girls side, there were Ogie, Okie, Ocie, Oma (who was called Omie and pronounced Oh-me) , Opal Pearl who went by the name Elizabeth and another sister named Orie Lee who only lived about nine months. On the boys side, there were Oliver who was called Ollie, Otto who was my father and of course Raleigh.

Because I was named after my father, everyone in my immediate and extended family called me Junior which they pronounced "June-your" and I absolutely hated being called that as long as I can remember.

I know hate is a strong word but I hated being called Junior so much that when I was 15 years old, I demanded my family start calling me by my given name which is Otto.

As you can imagine, after calling me Junior for 15 years, I had to remind some of my family members a few times; but they eventually honored my wishes and started calling me Otto like my friends, my classmates in school, and everyone else.

Most of the time, we humans don't understand why we like what we like and why we dislike what we don't. Most people don't make the time or find the value in getting quiet enough to allow their thoughts and mind to slow down enough to have the answers to their biggest life questions appear from what seems like "out of nowhere."

It's not always easy and the answers aren't always what you most want to hear, but what I've found time and time again to be true is when I get quiet, the answers almost always appear, sometimes in miraculous ways.

With that being said, you're probably not surprised to learn that when I started asking myself and the Universe why I hated being called Junior so much, the answers did come. You'd think those reasons would have been more complicated than they turned out to be, but they weren't. The reason I hated the name Junior and why I didn't want to be called that anymore turned out to be simple. In fact, it turned out to be so drop-dead simple that you don't have to be a rocket scientist or an armchair amateur psychologist to get it.

As I was growing up, I thought there were only two names you could call your kids that were worse than being called Junior and these names were Bubby or Bub if you were a boy, and Sissy or Sis if you were a girl. In my opinion, if being called Junior was bad, Bubby, Bub, Sissy and Sis were worse.

I know this is just my thinking that I made up, but other than the now retired Hall of Fame, former Major League Baseball player, Ken Griffey, Jr, I'd never seen or heard of a single person who was called Junior who seemed to be smart and making the best use of his God-given talents and abilities to create the best life possible for himself.

I recall thinking about full grown men who were called Junior like Junior Davis, Junior Tackett, and Junior

Whitaker and thinking, "What a waste," and "What a disgrace."

Why would full grown men put up with being called Junior?

I wouldn't and I didn't.

When I unpack my hatred for the name Junior and the names Bubby, Bub, Sissy and Sis, several things come to mind. The first is these are all "hillbilly" names that only poorly-educated, lower class moms and dads from the mountains would use when addressing their children.

Part of this must have come from my thinking that my father and mother are from the mountains of Kentucky, my father only had a sixth grade education and seemed to have more difficulty reading and writing than most other people. Other than reading the newspaper and the Bible, I never saw my father read any other book or magazine for pleasure or education.

Another reason I disliked the name Junior so much is because of my thinking that if you are named after your father and called Junior, you are not a complete or whole person. As I saw it, if you were called Junior because you were named after someone else, that meant you were an apprentice person who could only hope to learn how to become a legitimate, fully whole, and valuable person someday. Not today, but someday.

Again, I totally understand this is only my thinking at work here and it would be so easy to think that the main reason I hated the name Junior so much is because of where our family is from, what our heritage is, and what most people are like that are from there.

It would also be so easy to draw the conclusion from all this that the reason I hated the name Junior so much is because I was embarrassed by what I perceived my father Otto, Sr.'s many faults, shortcomings and deficiencies were.

While that may have been part of it, I've discovered there is something much bigger at play here which leads to another interesting and important question.

Because my given first name, Otto, is such an unusual name and isn't common in the USA where I live and because a name like this is ripe with possibilities for being made fun of, you might be wondering if I dislike the name Otto as well.

The answer is both yes and no. I like the name Otto because it's so different and it's easy to remember but I dislike like it greatly for other reasons.

When my first wife was pregnant with our son, she wanted to name him after me and have him be Otto Collins, III. I quickly put the brakes on that thought. I know that kids are kids but they can also be brutal in their teasing and name-calling. I didn't want our son to go through what I went through in the name-calling department. I didn't want other kids to shout out to him in the hallway at school, "Hey Otto, get your finger out of your exhaust," or call him things like "auto-matic", "auto-lotto", or "auto-mobile" either.

It's totally true that if they want to, kids can find anything to tease another kid about if they look hard enough or find the right button to push. I didn't want to voluntarily name our kid something that is just a setup for what I thought could be a lot of potential disrespect.

So the compromise my son's mother and I made was there'd be no Otto Collins III and we'd name our son after my best friend at the time and Otto would be his middle name.

The reason I didn't want my son to be called Otto or Junior was because of my own self-hatred that had manifested and come alive through my own thinking about my names. I figured if my son had self-hatred issues, I didn't want it to be because of me or my name. He'd have to find some other reason to beat himself up that didn't involve this.

Perhaps my hatred of the name Junior didn't have anything to do with my father and the fact that that I was named after him. Maybe It didn't have anything to do with hillbillies, education, intelligence, or wealth or anything else that I associated with the name either.

What if my issues around all this have simply been a function of my thinking and how much or how little I've loved myself?

What if all the fault I was finding with myself, my father and my life was only my resistance to seeing myself as a good, whole, perfect, just-as-I-am spiritual being and had nothing to do with the name itself?

What if my hatred for the name was simply a signpost pointing the way to my own healing I just hadn't found or embraced yet?

What if my whole life path was just like everyone else's path which is one life and one spiritual lesson after the next on the way to self-acceptance and self-love and a way seeing my own divinity, perfection and worthiness for having an even greater life.

Maybe it's time I start to see the name Junior as simply a name and not all the things I've made up about it.

Maybe it's time I start to see my perfection and divinity and live from this place more of the time.

Maybe it's time for you to start looking for more of this in your life as well.

"How you choose to see things
governs what shows up."

Richard Bartlett

Author of *The Physics of Miracles*

Chapter 8
Stay and Have Dinner with Us

We have a reason for everything we do in life and one of the things that used to drive me crazy about my father was how much, how often, and with whom he would utter the words:

"Stay and have dinner with us."

He did this his entire life.

During his younger years, if someone stopped by our house to pay us a visit on the weekend or a holiday when he wasn't working at the foundry or getting ready to preach somewhere, no matter what time of the day, my father would ask them to stay and have dinner with us. In his later years, when he wasn't working and had more time, family, friends, and church members would stop by for a visit any day of the week and as always, he'd say to them before their visit was over, "Stay and have dinner with us."

With disgust, I watched him do this hundreds of times and of course not everyone would take him up on his offer, but he almost always made the offer. Time and time again, both as a boy and later as a man, I would cringe when he made his invitation.

It took me 40 years to understand why I hated him doing this so much and just as long to understand why he did it.

Maybe the reason I didn't like my father inviting all these people to dinner was because I didn't like some of these people very well. Maybe I didn't like it when I was young was because I didn't want to have to be on my best behavior. At dinner time, I could just act normal, whatever that was, if we didn't have company. Or maybe the reason I hated his invitations so much was because I worried about how much or how little money or food we had in the house.

My mother and father always struggled financially. When my sister and I were older, my father may have just borrowed some money from one of us before extending an invitation to others. I didn't think it was very smart to be giving away places at the dinner table when they needed help to make ends meet themselves.

In our family, while I was growing up, we ate most of our meals at home, rarely eating out.

In fact, I had no memory of my family eating at a restaurant until I was 12 years old; but when I checked with my sister, she said we indeed went to a restaurant as a family once or twice a year on special occasions like a birthday or when we were on a trip.

We would go to Morton's Restaurant at the corner of Eleventh and Chillicothe Streets or to the Town House Restaurant on Sixth Street, right across from Martings, which was our city's only high-end department store.

We'd also eat out when we made the two-hour car trip from our home in Portsmouth to visit my Grandmother Collins and Uncle Raleigh in the mountains near Prestonsburg, Kentucky. On these trips, we'd stop at the Bluegrass Restaurant in Ashland, Kentucky.

This was a drive-in restaurant and even though this was the 1970s, it may as well have been the 1950s because when you went there, it was like going back in time. The servers at the Bluegrass were actually car-hops who'd bring your food on a tray that would attach to your car door window by two large aluminum hooks. Every time we'd stop there, my dad would have what he called the biggest hamburger he'd ever seen.

These were rare treats that were few and far between and probably one of the reasons I love to eat out at restaurants so much today.

Rich Bread, Poor Bread

There was something else that happened that probably had quite a bit to do with me not approving of my father inviting friends, family members and in some cases, total strangers to stay and have dinner with us and it was this:

My sister Ruth, who is 7 years older than me, has been married to her first and only love Walter (Lee to most of us) for over 40 years. They got married about six weeks after my sister's 16th birthday by the Reverend Jimmy Williams on New Year's Day in our living room.

Lee comes from a big family of ten kids, seven boys and three girls. His dad, Scotty, worked as an *I'll-do-whatever-you-need-me-to-do-for-not-very-much-money* janitor at the local Salvation Army.

While most people think of the Salvation Army as an organization that helps people in need when disasters both big and small strike, there was another side to the Army.

They held church services on Sunday mornings and I would go to them on occasion after spending the night with two of Lee's brothers, Chris and Larry.

About Tuesday or Wednesday on those weeks, Chris, Larry and I would petition my mom and dad to let me skip going to church the next Sunday morning with them and let me go to the Sunday morning service at the Salvation Army.

While I've always liked Chris and Larry a great deal and enjoyed spending time with them, there was another reason I liked to go to the Sunday morning church services at the Salvation Army.

It was the breads.

There was a bakery about a mile away called the Sixth Street Bakery and another one called Mrs. Renison's Original Crispie Creme Doughnut Shoppe and both of these businesses would donate the biggest assortment of cakes, pies, rolls, doughnuts and breads you'd ever seen to the Salvation Army every Saturday after they closed for the week.

The church would then give them away to anyone who attended the Sunday morning service and believe me when I say I wanted them.

The cakes, pies, rolls and doughnuts they gave away were great but the thing that always stood out to me were the breads.

At our house, we had two kinds of bread—white and yellow. My mother would make cornbread that we'd have with our dinners and sometimes she's also make fried white cakes of bread she'd fry up in a cast iron skillet. The bread we'd eat with our sandwiches was white bread that my dad would get at the local Dolly Madison surplus store on Tuesdays because it was always cheaper that day.

This is why it was unusual for me to see all those different kinds of bread and none of them were white. The Salvation Army had wheat, rye, pumpernickel, sourdough, cinnamon swirl and many others but what I couldn't figure out was why I'd never seen these breads in my life since they all tasted so good.

This is the way it is so often in life. You don't know what you don't know and here's what I didn't know about all these different varieties of bread that I'd come to enjoy so much.

Because these breads were being given away to people less fortunate, I thought they were somehow not as good quality and were breads that poor people typically ate. Call it just plain ignorance but after a while, I finally caught on to the fact that THESE breads were not the breads for poor people. They were more expensive, higher quality breads that people with more money than us would typically buy.

My father always worked hard and we never went hungry but we certainly weren't wealthy and then in that moment of realization, the truth set in.

Now I knew.

When I had this aha moment, it the first time I realized we were not a family of means.

And what did I do with this new information?

I did what everyone does in every moment.

I made up story after story about what this meant: who I was as a person, who we were as a family, and what you should or shouldn't do if you did or didn't have money. I made up stories about what was possible for my future, who I'd be able to date, who I'd marry, where I'd live and on and on. The trouble with the stories I made up in my head was that none of them were true. That's why they're called stories, because stories are things we've made up.

When it came to my father, it took me 40 years to realize that whether I thought it was okay or not for him to invite all these people to stay and have dinner was nothing more or less than what I thought and my opinions about what I thought.

We never had this conversation but I'm imagining that if I had asked him why he invited all these people to stay and have dinner with us all the time, I bet he would have told me that's what you do when you love people, care about them, and want to treat them with kindness. Even if he didn't have much himself, inviting friends and family to dinner was *his* way of showing love.

There was a navy blue plaque with a silver wire coil frame around it that hung on my parents' wall for 30 years and it simply said, "The Lord will provide." This is something my father truly believed. It was something he lived and something that he had proven to himself time and time again.

I know this because of how he lived.

This was something I hadn't learned yet and now I just smile when I think about how he was with other people even though I thought he would have been far better off if he'd made different choices.

I spent so much time, effort and energy judging him, making him wrong, thinking about and telling him what he should or shouldn't do all because of what I thought.

I've learned that we all have innate wisdom that's operating within us all the time.

My father's inner wisdom told him to invite people to dinner as an act of kindness and love and if he did, God would take care of him.

For many years I thought my father had no business inviting people to stay and have dinner with us all the time. Now I see that it was just his way of showing and giving love.

How could I make him wrong for that?

"Everything that happens to you has spiritual significance."

Rick Warren

Author of *The Purpose Driven Life*

Chapter 9
Rattlesnakes in the Cemetery

"Watch out for rattlesnakes" was the first thing that got my attention on that hot summer day in the mountains of Kentucky. These were the words my Uncle Raleigh shouted out to me when I was already ten minutes into cutting waist-high weeds with a long razor-sharp machete.

A few minutes earlier, he'd given me the huge knife as we started climbing up the steep hill leading to the cemetery where my father's parents and a lot of my other family members on the Collins side are buried.

The second thing that got my attention on that day was a lot more subtle but in time, it changed everything about how I saw what my father's life was like when he was growing up.

My son, Steven, was 12 years old at the time and since he was out of school for the summer and spending some time with me, I thought this would be the perfect time for him to learn about his roots and some of our family history. I also thought my mom and dad would like some extra time with just us boys.

So I decided we'd get up early on that Saturday morning and Steven and I would drive the fifty miles to pick up my mom and dad in Portsmouth. Then the four of us would drive another two hours into the mountains of eastern Kentucky to visit my Uncle Raleigh who still lives in the house where he, my father and their siblings grew up.

It was also our opportunity to pay a visit to other family members at their final resting place, the Collins Cemetery at East Point Kentucky.

After we picked up my Uncle Raleigh and went to the cemetery, my mom and dad decided that the hill was too steep for them to climb in their current levels of health. So, with that decision, my son Steven, my Uncle Raleigh, and I took a run at the hill with machetes and weed eaters in hand.

We went straight up the hill, through the gate of the chain link fence and into the cemetery, spending a half hour clearing weeds and brush. I think my uncle asked for my help that day not only because he was the self-appointed caretaker of the cemetery, but also he'd had a run-in with an unfriendly family of rattlesnakes there a few weeks before.

After our chores were over, we paid our respects to our family members that I both knew and didn't know and skidded our way back down the hill to rejoin my mother and father.

The next part of our day-long adventure was a life-changer for me.

We'd only been driving a few miles on dirt country roads when my father asked me to pull over and when I did, he got out of the car and walked around. At first I couldn't see any reason why he had asked me to stop the car because it looked like we were about as far into the woods as we could get and still be close to civilization.

That's when my father pointed with his right hand toward an opening between two big hills and said, "Back there is where I lived for the first few years of my life." Then, he turned around and pointed to an old, run-down wooden building that was about two hundred feet away and said, "That was the school building I went to school in until I had to quit before going into the sixth grade."

I just couldn't fathom it. I couldn't imagine how anyone could learn anything in that building. This old dilapidated one-room school house was smaller than apartments I've lived in. There was no indoor plumbing and it wasn't big enough to have multiple classrooms which meant that all the grades had to be taught in the same room at the same time.

And how did the kids get there? The only way had to be on foot and I'd be willing to bet there wasn't anything like a "snow day" where the kids didn't have to go to school because of bad weather.

On that day, I understood my father in a way I'd never understood him before.

I got to see how he truly grew up, what his life was like and what a hard life really was. I got clear that his life growing up had nothing to do with the life that he tried to give my sister and me. I saw very clearly I had made up a lot of stories about how hard my life was without really knowing what he had been through.

On that day, looking out at that rundown one-room schoolhouse, I also understood and gained a peace about something that had been running in the background of my mind, bothering me since my senior year in high school.

It was the story about how unprepared I was to go to college and how it was my parents' fault and specifically my father's fault. I remember being in the twelfth grade in high school and hearing all my friends, one by one, talk about this college or that university they'd applied to or been accepted. At some point, I finally caught on to the reality that my friends and their parents had been preparing for the next part of their lives which was college all along.

But I wasn't.

I can't ever remember my mom, dad, or a school counselor suggesting that I attend college. Maybe they did and I had some kind of selective memory about it but I don't remember any conversations like that.

Because of this and my own lack of foresight, I was clueless about how important college and learning was. I thought that when high school came and went, that was it. You finish school and then you get a job and live your life.

When I woke up to the fact that I'd been left behind, I thought I was screwed and had missed my chance to have a great life. I thought I wouldn't be able to have all the finer things because I didn't value a college education or education in general.

When I realized that all the other kids in my school were being prepared to go to college by both their parents and the school and I wasn't, I felt alone, embarrassed, and in some ways afraid of what the future would hold for me without a college degree.

In my mind, I immediately wanted to find someone to blame and I didn't look any further than my father. I thought after all, a father is supposed to prepare his son to face the world and be able to win and in that moment, I didn't think my father had done a very good job of preparing me to win after high school.

Fast-forward 20 years later and the day-trip that was supposed to be informative and educational about our family for my son turned into one of the most healing experiences of my life regarding my father and to some degree my mother too.

On that day, standing there watching my father point at that old one-room schoolhouse, all of those thoughts, images, and disappointments I had held against him all melted away.

I realized that for my parents, my graduating from high school was a big deal and I'm sure they thought it was a bigger accomplishment than I did. I'm assuming they thought this because neither of them had graduated from high school and I was the first in our family to do so.

Maybe that's why my mom and dad got dressed up in their "Sunday best" and applauded and cheered all through the ceremony, sporting smiles the entire day.

Today, I know how ridiculous all of this is and I recognize this was just my thinking run rampant because I did end up going to college. For that period of time, my fears and embarrassments about not being prepped for higher education like my friends was very real.

It took me 20 years and a flash of insight on a backwoods country road to see how much my parents loved me back then, how proud they were of me, and how much they saw possibilities for me that I didn't and couldn't see for myself at that time, whether I ever went to college or not.

I'm glad I was finally able to let all of that go.

"It's the gymnasium of life where you get the workout, the resistance, and you find out things about yourself that you did not know."

Bishop T. D. Jakes

Author of *Healing the Wounds of the Past*

Chapter 10
You Love Me, Don't You?

I was talking with my dad on the phone one night several years before he died and he said something that totally shocked me.

The reason it shocked me wasn't so much what he said but who was saying it and how he was saying it.

As first, I didn't understand the depth of what he was asking or why he would even ask me such a question because I thought he of all people should know the answer.

His question that he would ask a couple of hundred times in the final years of his life was:

"You love me, don't you?"

The first time he asked, I thought he was joking because he asked in a way a beggar in the street might ask for money—embarrassed and ashamed of how far he had fallen in life.

When he first asked me the question, I felt like he was trying to beckon something out of me that didn't want to come out. Something I wasn't willing to show him or open up to.

I've thought a lot over the years about why I was so angry with him in those moments when he tried to force me to tell him that I loved him. I also wondered why I wanted to withhold this gift because he simply wanted me to say the words, "Yes, I love you."

These were big questions with no easy answers and it took months for me to realize why I was acting this way—unable or unwilling to give my dad the gift he really wanted which was simply to tell him I loved him.

I finally understood the problem was that it was too difficult and too painful for me to see the strong man I knew and in many ways, unconsciously idolized, turn into someone else. This felt like weakness to me and the dad I knew was anything but weak. The version of him I was used to keeping in my head was him as a strong, forceful, dominant man who wasn't afraid of anything.

The version of him I liked to keep in my head was of the man at 30 and 40 years old who worked all day at the foundry, went to church after work to preach a sermon to try to save a few souls, and then went to his second job as a janitor at the K & M Restaurant at night after the restaurant closed. He would then get up and do it again.

The version of him I liked to keep in my head was him at 81 years old killing a copperhead snake that had just fallen out of a tree with nothing more than a garden hoe one hot summer day, while he and my mother were visiting my Aunt Becky.

But by now, other than a few isolated events, that version of him was fading and being replaced by a man with more simple needs like wanting to know he was loved by the people he cared about the most.

I don't know what happened but one day I got an insight that shifted everything around this issue with my father.

I wondered:

What if I could lay down my ideas of him as strong or weak?

What if I could show him kindness without resistance?

What if I could love him and give him the thing he wanted most in those moments—to let him know that he was loved by me?

And with those insights or questions, everything shifted for me, not only with my dad, but with the other people in my life as well.

I'd always been able to tell the women in my life that I loved and cared about them but this was new and different. Now, I felt a certain sense of freedom around this issue and felt much more love for the other people who came and went in my life, even total strangers, that I hadn't felt before. I was learning to live as love with everyone I'd meet and in a strange way, I think this helped me have an even better relationship with my son.

It also helped me to be the kind of man who could be both strong enough *and* vulnerable enough to allow my son to tell me he loves me so openly and freely at an age that I wasn't able to with my father.

I've read hundreds of books, attended hundreds of seminars and have been coached by and studied with many of the top leaders in the world of self-development. My intention was to discover what one writer, teacher or philosopher after another had to share that could help me become the best version of myself I could possibly be.

In 1997, I read a book by the singer-songwriter, Kenny Loggins, and his wife at the time, Julia, called *The*

Unimaginable Life that totally rocked my world and gave me a new sense of possibility around relationships.

There's a line in the book that had such a lasting effect on me where Kenny said,

"We ALL long for love. Everything else in life is just killing time."

I agree and apparently, so did my father.

It might seem like a strange thing in today's world for me to say this and to be quoting one of the most famous singer-songwriters of my generation, but I'm willing to bet, my father and I aren't the only men or women who have longed for and desired to have BIG love in their lives. I'm also willing to bet that most men and women want their hearts, minds, bodies and souls to be even more filled up with love than what they're experiencing right now.

The trouble is most people don't realize the love they want is already inside them and it's been there all along. They don't have the love they want because without realizing it, they spend most of their days, weeks, and lives doing the very things that cut themselves off from love.

This is tragic and leads me to ask a couple of simple questions that are worth spending a few quiet moments alone pondering:

Could there be places within you or things you do that keep love away?

Could you be the one putting up invisible roadblocks to the love or the life you want?

These are certainly questions worth considering and as I bring this chapter to a close, I can't help but wonder what our lives would be like if men and women could put down the armor they use to protect themselves and their hearts and open more to love in every moment.

It makes me wonder what life would be like for us if we could tell the people in our lives what they mean to us more of the time without them needing to prompt us or guilt-trip us into it.

Of all the things that are important to us in life, perhaps the most important is knowing the answer to the question "Am I loved?" is a resounding "Yes."

When you consider your interactions and relationships with the people in your life, there's another question that's worth asking that may be just as important:

Am I giving love?

Openly?

Freely?

Boldly?

Courageously?

In my life, I have a terrific marriage with my wife, Susie and I also have many amazing friendships and relationships.

As much as I'd like to say I've got this down and I'm acting from this place of love all the time, it's just not true. I've spent way more time in my life holding back than I'm comfortable admitting. I'm also keenly aware I'm a work-in-progress, trying hard to answer "yes" to those questions, and live from a place of love and kindness as much of the time as possible.

I'm guessing there's a part of what I just said that describes you as well.

"We are wrongly led to believe that life makes us into the kind of person we are. In truth, it's our level of understanding that makes life what it is for us! This is why nothing can really change for us until we see that trying to change some condition in life without first changing the consciousness responsible for its appearance is like blaming the mirror for what we don't like seeing in it!"

Guy Finley

Author of *The Secret of Your Immortal Self*

Chapter 11
No Shirt, No Shoes, No Shorts

Most of us think convictions are solid, unchanging, immovable, and unwavering.

One of the things I could say about my father with total certainty is that he was a man of conviction—a man of principle. I didn't always agree with or think his way was the right way for me, but he lived according to his convictions and I appreciated that about him.

My father didn't drink, didn't smoke and I never heard him swear or say anything foul or inappropriate. Although I'm sure my parents' relationship wasn't perfect, I never heard or saw him do anything that would have been considered a betrayal of my mother.

In my entire life, I never saw my father wear a pair of short pants or a short-sleeved shirt in public. Even on the hottest days, if he was working at the foundry, in the garden, or on some project at home, he wore long work pants and long-sleeved work shirts. When he wasn't working, he almost always wore dress pants, a perfectly ironed long-sleeved dress shirt and either dress or casual shoes. I don't think he owned a pair of tennis shoes in his life. He never went to a theater to see a movie. His hair was cut every two weeks and he never wore a beard.

I think there were two possible reasons why he was strict on himself and unwavering about how he looked and how he acted. The first was that these convictions and commitments could have been ways for him to work through his pain of not having much as a child while growing up. The second reason for these very strict and unnecessary guidelines for living came from his belief that since he was a man of God, this is how God would want him to dress, act, and behave.

Hundreds of times, I heard him say, "Your word has got to be your bond." To me that meant to be honest, to say what you intend to do, and keep your word. As far as I could see, he really tried to live by these words.

Sometimes I had to look closely to see it but over the years, I enjoyed how much he grew, evolved, and changed. I enjoyed seeing him live according to his convictions and at the same time start to open to other's points of view and experiences. He started to allow other people to have their own experience without making them wrong.

For example, Della, one of my dad's nieces, was married to Chester and they had children together. While Della and Chester were still married, Della's sister, Judy, also had children with Chester. They were all living together under the same roof with my dad's sister, Elizabeth, and her husband, Clinton. I know this sounds like something you'd read on the internet or see on a bad reality TV show, but it's totally true.

As all of this was unfolding, my father, as well as his older brother, Ollie, were totally livid and let their sister Elizabeth and the entire family know just how wrong they thought their living situation was. My dad and his brother accused them of "living in sin."

For the longest time, my dad tried to get them to see how wrong this was and spent a lot of time and energy trying to get them to change their ways, but it never happened. Because of this, my dad's relationships with his sister and especially the nieces were strained to say the least.

Thirty years passed. My dad's sister, Elizabeth, died during that time. One day my dad happened to be at an extended family function where he saw Della. Sensing how much judgment my dad still had about this situation, Della said to him, "I don't know why you have a problem with the way we're living, if we don't have a problem with it."

After that, my father must have seen something different and softened toward the situation. He still didn't approve of how they were living, but after she said that, he was kinder toward her and the rest of their family.

Back in my world, I was really afraid of how my father was going to react when my first marriage was ending after fifteen years. After all, my father's opinion was something I highly valued and like most men, I wanted his approval and love—even if I wasn't conscious of how much I wanted it until later in my life after many deep moments of introspection.

My father believed when you made the commitment to get married, you got married for life and you didn't abandon ship when the waves of life and love come crashing in on you. You tough it out and figure it out. That's what he saw in his family growing up and that's how he lived.

That's why it was such a surprise to me when he met me with total love and acceptance when I made the decision to leave my ex-wife.

I don't remember my dad and me talking about the particulars of what went into my decision to leave my marriage. I don't remember any late night conversation about how the passion, spark, and connection was gone between my ex and me. I don't remember telling him that with the exception of my ex and I agreeing how important it was important to raise our son to be a good person, she and I were two people on completely different paths in life.

What I do remember in the dynamics between my dad and me was the seismic shift from how I thought he would react to my first marriage breaking up to how he actually did react.

He reacted with love and a sense of solidness that seemed to silently say without the need for words, "I'm here for you, son. I'm here."

Most people think their convictions are fixed and are strong enough to take them through their entire lives, but I haven't found that to be true. I've found there are very few things in our lives we'd consider convictions so strong and so powerful that they would truly stand up to the "I'd-never-do-THAT-no-matter-what" test.

In this case, I'm so glad my dad was able to see past his long-held convictions about love, marriage and divorce and just love me anyway.

But, if he hadn't been able to open his heart to me and find it in him to love me anyway, I can now see that it would have been my job to love him no matter what and find that place of unconditional love within me that I had hoped for from him.

Growing, changing, and evolving is deep, soul-stirring work and most of the time we don't and can't see growth and change, both in ourselves and in others happening in the moment; but what I've come to see is that it is almost always happening whether we're aware of it or not.

Yes, my father had deep personal and spiritual convictions but life worked on him so much that in time, change, compassion and love became his friends as well.

"A miracle is a shift in perception from fear to love—from a belief in which is not real, to faith in that which is. That shift in perception changes everything."

Marianne Williamson

Author of *A Return to Love*

Chapter 12
The Miracle

I used to think the idea of a "miracle" was nonsense and for most of my life, I thought true miracles don't happen, especially to me and to the people I know, love or care about. I thought miracles were somehow reserved for special or chosen people.

And then one day a miracle happened to my dad and I've been a believer ever since.

There are different kinds of miracles in life. There are physical, emotional, spiritual, relationship, financial and many other kinds of miracles. My father's was physical. It was dramatic and it was life-changing.

Compared to my father, I've been a total wimp in the pain department. If my back is out of alignment or my body is a little bit sore from sleeping in a weird position or doing a little bit of yard work, I'm off as quickly as I can to the chiropractor or massage therapist to get my body feeling good again. I can't imagine what it would be like to be in constant, excruciating pain like my father was for the last 40 years of his life.

My dad worked as a laborer at a foundry for 21 years and it was hard, physical work. He was part of a team with another man for eight to ten hours a day. Their job was to bend down and turn over three hundred pound molds that had been poured with molten iron earlier in the day. After they turned over these heavy molds, the finished part would fall out onto the floor to cool off. Then the part would be prepared to be shipped to the manufacturer who had placed the order.

One day several years into his employment with the foundry, my father bent down to pick up one of these heavy molds like he'd done thousands of times before but this time he didn't get up. Two of the discs in his vertebrae slipped out of place and he collapsed on the ground in excruciating pain, beginning a lifetime of back pain.

In those days, they didn't have lasers and different types of technology for healing the body from injuries like we have today. So my dad spent 36 days in traction, which is essentially a process of stretching the vertebrae in your back in an attempt to get the discs between the vertebrae to go back in the slots where they belong.

With my father, it didn't work and even though he never lost his drive or work ethic, he would never physically be the same after that injury.

It was a good thing the foundry foreman liked my dad. When he was finally able to go back to work, they found him another job working new machines that were compliant with the doctor's orders of light duty work. I wouldn't have called these machines light duty but my dad could do the work and that's what he did for the last part of his 21 years at the Portsmouth Casting company.

My father's health problems didn't stop there. After his sister, Elizabeth, died, he had a series of light strokes and after a while found himself in a wheelchair where he stayed for seven and a half years. He simply wasn't the same man he used to be. His health had declined so much that Dave Conley became not only his friend but also his caretaker. I was living away during this time and was not aware of or unconsciously chose to ignore how serious my father's heath issues were.

Seven and a half years is a long time to have to endure anything you don't want to do but being confined to a wheelchair was the burden my father had to bear until the miracle happened.

Here's how I remember it:

My sister, Ruth, and brother-in-law, Lee, were living six hours away at the time and would make the journey to visit my mom and dad, Lee's parents, as well as other family and friends as often as possible.

During these weekend visits, Lee liked to play cards with his brothers on Saturday nights and sometimes he would be out quite late enjoying his time at the card table. One of those Saturday nights they were in town, Ruth, who is a very sound sleeper, was asleep on the pullout couch in the front room of our parents' house. It was four o'clock in the morning and Lee was still out when all of a sudden, my sister heard a loud noise, like the sound of someone trying to open the door and break in. She then started screaming, "NO, NO, NO! Get Out! Get Out!"

When my father who was in bed in the next room heard all this screaming, a protective instinct kicked in for my sister and he got out of bed, totally forgetting that he'd been confined to a wheelchair for so long. He took two or three steps and crashed to the floor, hurting his hip pretty badly in the process.

The way I remember this story is that this was the first time he had taken steps by himself in over seven years and it was the catalyst for him believing he could walk again. Before long, he was out of the wheelchair and walking on his own.

That's right, wheelchair gone, walking on his own without help from anyone.

For years, I thought this story was true and as it turns out, it's NOT true. Apparently I had made it all up. Recently, when I checked with Ruth and my mother about all of this, they didn't remember my dad's miracle happening like that at all.

Their version went something like this:

One morning my dad, Mom, Ruth and a couple of others were sitting at the table having breakfast when my father smiled and all of a sudden got up out of his wheelchair and started walking.

No big drama. Nobody screaming around. No one thought anyone needed rescuing from a would-be burglar. None of that!

My mother simply thinks that on that morning when they were all sitting around the breakfast table God touched my father's body and healed him. From that moment on, my dad left the wheelchair behind. He no longer needed it. He was indeed healed. There's no other explanation for it.

It was a true miracle.

So, dear reader, which is true?

I don't know.

What I do know is that most of life's experiences are totally made up in our heads and our memories are made up of our thoughts. For example, whether I think my father was a good father or a bad one because he never attended any of my little league baseball games when I was a kid is all made up.

We have a fact—my father never once attended any of my baseball games when I was in little league. Then we have what I made up about what that meant—that a good father attends his son's baseball games and a bad father doesn't.

Whether my son would choose to think I was a good father or a bad one because I left his mother and broke the family up is totally and completely made up.

Again, we have the fact—I left my son's mother when he was eight and the three of us were no longer together as a family. Then we have whatever he believes about his thinking about this truth. Everything else is totally and completely made up.

The fact is that a miracle really did happen in my father's life. He really did get up, start walking places and driving a car again after being in a wheelchair for so many years. The story I told myself and believed about how all of this happened turned out to *not* be true.

I said earlier in this chapter that there are many different kinds of miracles and I've experienced many.

Marianne Williamson, the author of the books, *A Return to Love* and *Tears to Triumph,* once said that a miracle is simply a shift in perception. When I think of my father, my wife, my extended family, my friends, and other relationships in my life, I've experienced many shifts in perception that have changed those relationships and my life for the better—often permanently.

The key to a miracle happening in your life is seeing things differently.

The key to seeing things differently is a measure of how open you are to seeing something new in each interaction and in each moment with the people in your life and your state of mind in each moment.

The shifts in perception I've had about my dad that I've shared in this book, as well as others I haven't shared, have produced miracles in my life. I love the fact that I've had these and I'm open to more.

"What if God was one of us?
Just a slob like one of us
Just a stranger on the bus
Tryin' to make his way home?"

From the song "One of Us"

Performed by Joan Osborne

Chapter 13
The Final Gift

"I don't think I'm going to make it," my father said to me as he laid in his hospital bed that Wednesday morning.

I'd heard him say these words a few times before and I either didn't take him seriously, I didn't understand what he was trying to say, or I simply didn't fully understand what he was going through in those moments.

This time, however, it felt different. It felt real.

He'd been sent by ambulance the day before to one of the best hospitals in the country. It was a 90 mile drive for the ambulance driver but only a mile from where Susie and I were living at the time. A few days before, he had fallen and hit his head on the bathroom sink on the way down.

At first, my father's injuries from the fall didn't seem too serious but my mother and sister convinced him to go to the small, local hospital anyway. After a full battery of tests, they found that my father was bleeding internally, possibly had another light stroke and was in need of more help than they could provide. My father's condition deteriorated quickly for the next day and a half and a couple of things happened that let me know he was near the end.

First, I noticed how much attention he was getting from doctors, nurses and specialists that you don't normally get when a condition isn't serious.

The second was that angels came for a visit right there in his hospital room. Maybe no one else felt them like I did that afternoon but for me, it was very real. The only explanation was there had to have been angels among us, ready to help and comfort us.

My mother, my sister, Susie, and I were gathered around a doctor for a mini-consulting session in the space next to my dad's bed. As the doctor was laying out his rather bleak prognosis for my father's short-term future, I decided to close my eyes, trying to be in the present moment as best I could, and listen to what the doctor had to say.

As I was standing there with my eyes closed, I felt the warm touch of a hand on my shoulder and back. It was one of the most beautiful and calming feelings I've ever felt and for whatever reason, I assumed my brother-in-law who had been sitting across the room had gotten up to join us and had put his hand on me. I'm not sure why it was important in that moment, but I opened my eyes to see if it was Lee at my back, but it wasn't him. He hadn't moved. He was still sitting in the chair across the room against the wall a few feet from the foot of my dad's hospital bed.

I'd heard about these kinds of things happening many times before where a guide, an angel or some other spiritual being comes calling to provided meaning or comfort at exactly the right moment and this felt like one of those moments.

To this day I can still feel what that angel's touch felt like. It was pure, beautiful, and healing. The physical sensation of the touch I felt sunk beyond my skin and into someplace deeper within me, perhaps all the way into that place beyond the body and into where the spirit lives.

The Gift

The next day was one I'll never forget.

It was August 29. It was my birthday. It was the day my dad died.

I don't remember his last words, but I do remember the day before when he was still able to talk. He asked Susie and I to pray for him.

He'd asked us to pray for him a few times before and each time I felt hesitant and uncomfortable. This was because my religious and spiritual beliefs were so different from his. I had judgment around the thought that if I started praying publicly—whether it was for him or a simply blessing our food at meal time—there would be questions from my parents about whether I was "saved" or not. This would be followed by endless invitations to go to church with them which I didn't want to do because of my differing beliefs.

I'd heard my father preach in churches many times over the years, especially in my younger years, about how we each have to find our own salvation and I'd done that in my own way. It just didn't agree with their way. I hadn't been able to say this in a way they could hear it yet.

Back in my dad's hospital room that day when he asked Susie and I to pray for him, something shifted within me and I let my judgments fall away about what it might mean and found a way to just love in that moment. We laid our hands on him and prayed for peace and comfort and for his journey to come.

My father's health continued to deteriorate quickly and there reached a point when his body was shutting down more and more by the hour and he could no longer speak.

At one point, one of the nurses asked us if it became necessary, did we want to put my father on life support. With my mother standing next to me, I turned to my father who couldn't speak and asked him if he wanted the help of the machines to keep him alive.

He simply shook his head no.

He'd had enough.

I got two gifts that morning:

The first was I was holding his hand when he died, just like he'd held mine many times before when I was young.

The second gift I received from him was something I mentioned earlier in this chapter. He died on my birthday. It's interesting to me to watch other people's reactions when they find out that he died on my birthday.

Their reactions usually fall into one of two camps:

1. "How sad (or terrible) that happened to you!" Or

2. "What a gift your father gave you!"

How you look at life is always a choice. It's a choice of whether to look at the day he died as a blessing or a cruel joke. It's based on what thoughts you're thinking and what thoughts you're attaching to in the moment.

The people who have the "How-sad-and-how-terrible-that-happened-to-you" reaction must think that my father somehow wronged me by leaving life in this way. These people must think that because of what happened, every birthday which is supposed to be special and filled with joy will be ruined for me from now on because he died on my birthday.

Fortunately, I'm not one of those people who see it this way. I see it as a special gift and not something to dread or a cruel joke.

Now, not only do I get to celebrate my special day each year any way I want, but I can choose to make it even more special by taking a moment to go within and say a little prayer of gratitude for this being the day that through him and my mother, I was born into the world at this particular time and space. It's also an opportunity for me to connect with the energy and spirit of my father who I think sometimes pays me short visits from the spirit world.

The Moment Time Stood Still

My father was gone.

His body was still here but his spirit, his essence, his soul was now able to soar into the heavens and return to the place we all come from before we are born into these bodies and begin our time in what Gary Zukav, author of the book, *Seat of the Soul*, called "earth school."

One by one we left my dad's hospital room, still stunned and in some ways relieved that my dad had passed.

What happened next was simply mind-blowing. I saw it as a sign that everything that had happened and everything that ever would happen in my life was in divine order, in the right timing and in the right way.

I also took what happened next as a sign that he, the angels, my father's spirit guides and our Creator were starting to mess with me a little bit and have some good old-fashioned fun at my expense.

After Dad died, a hospital official asked us to wait around for a few minutes to sign some papers. We all assumed those papers were about transporting his body the 90 miles back home to the funeral home we had chosen. A few minutes seemed to drag on for hours and we were getting more than a little fidgety and downright irritated. We were all tired. We'd been through a lot and we couldn't leave. We wondered what was going on.

More time went by and still no paperwork.

Finally a hospital representative came to see us with what we thought were the release papers but all she wanted to do was assure us that she was trying her best to get them for us and to make sure we weren't upset with the hospital. I assumed this was because we refused to put my father on life support but I don't really know.

Finally almost three hours later, someone arrived with the paperwork so we could bust my dad out of the hospital. My mother signed the papers and we were finally free to go. Glad all of this was finally over, feeling really hungry and thinking it must be past lunchtime, I looked down at my wristwatch.

How could this be?

My wristwatch said 11:09.

The problem was that it was well past 2:30 in the afternoon but my watch had stopped at 11:09 a.m. which was right before my dad died. When I saw that my watch had stopped cold right before his death, cold chills went up my spine and the hair stood up straight on the back of my neck.

Since I had been holding my dad's hand when he died, I couldn't help but wonder whether some kind of electrical charge went through his body and into mine and then into the watch causing it to stop less than thirty minutes before his death certificate says he took his last breath.

I'll never know what really happened to my watch on that day. What I do know is that on that morning of August 29, 2013, time really did stand still.

I'll never forget that moment and I wanted to find some way to remember it appropriately. I took a photo of my dad and me that had been taken two years before, put it in a small frame and pinned the watch inside so you can see the watch, my dad, and me as well as time standing still.

This picture hangs on my office wall where I'm writing this chapter as a way to honor our connection. It's also a tangible way to remember what happened on the day he died. The day that time stood still.

The Final Gift

My dad wasn't a sports fan at all.

He didn't care about the Reds, the Yankees, the Bears, the Kings, the Buckeyes, the Lakers, the Cowboys, the Maple Leafs, Real Madrid, Manchester United, Chelsea or any other sports team for that matter.

When I was growing up here in the United States, baseball, football and basketball were the most popular spectator sports and to my knowledge, my father never watched a game in its entirety in his life, either in person or on television.

He just wasn't interested—but I sure was.

I played baseball as a kid and I've attended live or watched on TV hundreds, possibly thousands, of sporting events throughout my lifetime.

Even though my dad wasn't interested in the games themselves, there was one thing he was interested in. The crowds. I would be watching a sporting event on TV and as he would walk through the room, he couldn't believe how many people were at those games. It was mind-blowing for him to see these huge crowds of 25,000, 50,000 or 100,000 people at an arena or a stadium.

He wouldn't sit and watch the game with me but would comment about how big the crowd was and how much he would love to preach to that many people. Being a country preacher, my dad was passionate about "bringing people to God." He preached in churches, in tent revivals, on the radio, to people and monkeys on the street and in city parks. He preached wherever and whenever he was called.

But as for his desire to preach to tens or hundreds of thousands of people in an arena or a stadium, it didn't happen in his lifetime. He never got his chance to make as big of an impact on others as he wanted.

Or did he?

When my father left this world, among other things, he left behind a wife who loved him and two fully grown adult children he could be proud of. He also left a legacy, perhaps a legacy much bigger than he ever dreamed possible. It was a legacy of love, kindness, generosity and service to the people he met as he traveled through life.

I said it earlier in this book and I'll say it again here, all my father wanted to do in this life was provide for his family in a way that his mother and father never could for him and to "serve the Lord" and serve others in a way that God would be proud of.

I think he did more than that!

When I think about my father's final gift, I have to wonder:

What if my father's final gift to me, to you, and to the world was simply his life and the fact that it was an example and not a warning?

What if my father's final gift and his legacy all happened after his death and this book was the vehicle through which he could minister to many and make a difference in their lives?

What if just talking about my father and how I came to see him differently could change the lives of fathers and sons all over the world as well as the people who love them?

I think these things are very real possibilities and here's an example of this in action:

A couple of years ago, I worked with a woman I'll call KW. She had twin boys who were quite a handful to say the least. One day we had a conversation about how my dad had died on my birthday and how we can choose to see it as a blessing or a curse.

I enjoyed talking with her that day but I didn't realize how much that conversation had meant to her until a year later. She told me her twin boys' father had died on their birthday when the boys were only three years old and that my telling her my dad's story had helped her more than I would ever know.

There's a famous line in the classic 1980 movie "The Blues Brothers" where Elwood Blues says in a totally deadpan way, "The Lord works in mysterious ways."

And I couldn't agree more.

Several years ago, I talked with a friend who told me about a conversation he'd had with an elderly gentleman who was close to death. My friend told me what this man shared with him and it's always stuck with me.

He said, "When you get to the end of your life and look back, *everything* will make perfect sense."

Now that I'm entering the second half of my life, I'm seeing more and more of the time just how true this is.

As I bring our time together in this book to a close, there's only one way that seems fitting to do it. It's to share my answer to a question my sister asked me recently at the funeral of my brother-in-law's mother, Francis, who our father loved and cared deeply about.

My sister asked me, "You know who would have loved to have been here, don't you?"

Without missing a beat, I said, "Our father," and after a pause, I said, "Who art in heaven."

With that, my sister simply smiled and seemed to appreciate my attempt at humor in the moment, knowing that if there really is such a place, our father is there and at the same time appreciating the gift that he'll always remain right here in our hearts.

"Your parents don't have to be alive to do 'The Work' on them. No one has to be alive for you to do The Work on them. They live in your mind. That's where you heal yourself."

Byron Katie

Author of *Loving What Is*

Chapter 14
The Little Red Chair

It was a September Sunday afternoon about three weeks after my father died. I was getting ready to leave after visiting my mother for a few hours when all of a sudden, she stopped me before I could get completely out the door. She cocked her head slightly upward and with sincerity and wanting in her voice she said, "Hold on. I have something I want to give you."

She turned around and shuffled into her bedroom, closing the door for a moment. She returned carrying the little red chair my father had promised me years earlier and offered up these words:

"Your dad wanted you to have this."

Not sure how to react, I felt stunned for a moment, like I'd been delivered some bad news or stepped through a doorway into a reality I'd not fully grasped. My father was gone but the chair remained and now I was being gifted with it. As I looked at the chair in that moment, I realized the finality of my dad's passing a little deeper.

I thanked my mother for the chair, turned and walked out the door. I put the chair in the back seat of my car, paused, and took a deep breath.

As I was driving back home, I remembered that some 40 years before, my father had promised me that little chair that took up space in every house we ever lived.

The chair wasn't the nicest looking thing I'd ever seen or the most practical. It was fire engine red with a 14 x 14 inch webbed seat and wooden slats for legs. It was obviously handmade. The chair was built for a small child but seemed to be important, almost holding a place of reverence in our home. This idea was strange because often I would find it in the most unusual places in our home.

It would appear in my parent's bedroom with old newspapers and magazines stacked on it. Occasionally, it sat proudly holding a freshly cleaned pair of my dad's dress shoes. Other times, the little red chair would be banished to a closet or a basement only to come out later like a toy or a locket that had long been forgotten and then rediscovered.

Over the years, I rarely thought about the chair. Even though somewhere in the back of my mind I knew the back story of the chair, I never truly knew the gravity of its importance to my father and that he wanted it to be mine someday until that Sunday afternoon.

What can a little red chair tell you about a man's life?

The answer is a lot if you pay attention and drop out of your preconceived thoughts, ideas and notions about what you think the man's life was like and you open to the story the chair would tell about him if it could.

I once had a conversation with my dad about his father and he said that because his father died when he was only two years old, he didn't have any memories of him at all. The only gift his father ever gave him was this little red chair, the chair that was passed on to me that afternoon many years later.

But what about the little red chair?

What made it special?

What was it that made it so important that my father made sure I knew that one day it would be mine?

The chair had to have been something more than just a small, handmade child's chair.

Although I never asked him, my guess is that it was a symbol for something my father wanted but never felt he had with his own father.

It's the same thing we all want but often find to be so elusive as we go through our lives—a sense of connection.

You don't have to have had a father, a grandfather or a brother to have a good life. And not having a father or a grandfather doesn't mean that something is missing. Those kinds of thoughts are stories we've made up about something that may be true or an event that's happened in our lives.

Connection is a feeling you have that comes from your thoughts about people, causes, events or specific moments in time you've deemed special and you want to hold onto.

Memories are made of moments in time we've made special. Most of the time, we don't realize these memories can be either good or bad, happy or sad, loving or not depending totally on our thinking in the moment about what those moments meant. They continue to be our memories only when we relive the thoughts about those people or situations and bring those thoughts into the present moment over and over again.

There's a line in the song, "The Hard Way," by the recording artist Mary Chapin Carpenter that I really like that speaks to what I've been talking about here.

It's the line where she sings, "We've got two lives, one we're given and the other one we make."

This was totally true about my father and the life he made for himself and our family. There was the life he was given and there was the life he made. I've always thought you can learn a lot about a man by watching him, seeing how he lives and what he makes important. In my father's life, there were two things that were more important than anything else—his God and his family.

When I was younger, I had a lot of complaints about my father that rolled around in my head. These were the remnants of all the millions of thoughts I had about how I thought he should have been different as a father and as a man.

These days, I have the gift of hindsight and when I think about what my father went through growing up, what most of his life was like, and the life he ended up making, I can't help but soften. I don't have to look very far or very long to find the good that he was.

I no longer see him as someone who could've or should've been different as a father or as a man. I see him these days as some kind of physical and spiritual badass that didn't cower, didn't quit, and didn't give up when life got hard for him, like so many people do.

When I was a young boy and my father told me he wanted me to have the little red chair one day, was this his way of asking me to stay connected and to remember him?

Maybe.

After my mother gave me the little red chair on that Sunday afternoon, wave after wave of emotion washed over me. In some strange way, I didn't feel like the chair was mine. I felt like I was a temporary steward appointed to watch over it for a time.

My son happened to be with me that Sunday that my mother gave me the chair and in that moment I turned to him and said the same thing my father said to me some 40 years earlier.

I said, "Son, someday this chair will be yours."

To that, he simply offered up a faint smile and said, "Thanks, Dad."

About the Author

Otto Collins is a relationship and life coach, author, speaker, spiritual teacher, seminar leader, businessman, and spiritual seeker who spends his time helping men and women all over the world tap into the love, spark and creative wisdom that's inside all of us all the time. Along with his wife, Susie, he is the co-author of over a dozen books and programs on love, relationships, and personal and spiritual growth including *Magic Relationship Words, Should You Stay or Should you Go?,* and *Stop Talking On Eggshells.*

For more info about Otto or to learn about his other books, audios, videos, coaching, consulting, seminars, classes, media appearances and everything else he's up to in the world visit:

OttoCollins.com

The Difference that Makes All the Difference in Life

A Personal Note from Otto:

For 84 years, my father struggled, strained and stressed himself out about all of life's problems both big and small.

No one should have to struggle like he did and if I could go back in time and gift my father with just one gift that would have made his life better in every single way—and knowing what I now know—I know exactly what I would do.

I'd go back in time and ask him if he was open to seeing some new possibilities for himself and his life and I'd show him what I've discovered over the past few years about where our life experience comes from.

I'd share with him how he could be happy on the inside, no matter what was going on in the outside world.

I'd show him how love, abundance, peace, happiness, success and prosperity are way more possible than most of us think, and not because of some special skill I could have taught him. I'd show him what I see about where everything we want in life comes from.

I'd ask my father to consider the possibility that the seeds for everything we want to have, be, or do in life is already inside of us. It's just that the thoughts in our head are sometimes so loud, negative and filled with fear that we take those thoughts as reality and don't step into the life we really want.

This is tragic but it's what happens in the lives of millions of men and women every day all over the world.

What if the challenges you face in love, life, or business were much easier to solve than you think?

What if one insight could make all the difference in the way you see the world?

What if your whole life could change for the better if you could only see things a little bit differently?

That's what could have been possible for my father and that's what is possible for you, if you can only learn what I call the difference that makes all the difference in life.

Whatever you're up against in life, whatever you want to change, improve, or be different all starts with seeing things differently. And seeing things differently comes from knowing the truth about where our experiences in life come from which is simply our thoughts and our thinking in the moment.

If there are any parts of your life that aren't working as well as you'd like, I invite you to reach out to me to see how I can help you.

In addition to the many books, courses, and programs that I've written and created with my wife, Susie that have helped thousands of people create better relationships and lives, I'm available for coaching and consulting with individuals, couples, businesses, and organizations.

Otto Collins

I offer relationship and marriage intensives for men, women, and couples and I also facilitate intensives, retreats, and seminars for groups and organizations of all sizes.

You can connect with me and learn more about my latest offerings at my website: OttoCollins.com

Blessings and Love,

Otto Collins

Things arint good or bad - only how they are percieved!

FREE Audio: For Fathers, Sons and the People Who Love Them

Discover why it's never too late to heal your relationship with your father, son, or anyone else. Learn why you can heal whatever differences you have with them even if they're no longer alive, even if they want nothing to do with you, and even if you don't know where they are. Let the healing begin...

Download or listen now at -- OttoCollins.com/NeverTooLate

Selected Books, Programs and Courses
By Otto and Susie Collins
(available at SusieandOtto.com)

Preaching to Monkeys
(paperback and audiobook)

Magic Relationship Words

Stop Talking on Eggshells

No More Jealousy

Should You Stay or Should You Go?

Relationship Trust Turnaround

Acknowledgements

To Sydney Banks for the 3 principles: Divine Mind, Divine Consciousness, and Divine Thought

To Michael Neill for Supercoach Academy and for being one of my guides along the way in life

To Mara Gleason for helping me to see that I'm OK, I've always been Ok, and I'll always be OK no matter what and it's just my thinking that would have me believe otherwise

To Gary Zukav for *Seat of the Soul*

To Michael Singer for *The Unthethered Soul and The Surrender Experiment*

To Stephen King for *On Writing*

To Lee Child for his *Jack Reacher* series which were not only fun books to read but in a strange way taught me how to write in a more compelling and engaging way

To Cathy Kline—Thanks for the superb job of editing this book and making it better

To Ruth, Lee, and my mother—Thanks so much for the love, support and kindness

To my father for being the best father and the best man you could possibly be while here in the physical world and for your love, support, guidance, and demands from the other side

Otto Collins

To my son Steven—Thanks so much for your love and for your encouragement to keep going in the early stages of writing this book and I'm glad you're my son

To my beloved Susie—No words could ever express how I feel about you or my appreciation for what you bring to my life. You're my spiritual soulmate and I've enjoyed every moment with you. Thanks also for what you've added to this book and project.

Made in the USA
Columbia, SC
07 August 2022

64823721R00074